RAND ARROYO CENTER

Malleability and Measurement of Army Leader Attributes

Personnel Development in the U.S. Army

Susan G. Straus, Tracy C. McCausland, Geoffrey Grimm, Katheryn Giglio

Prepared for the United States Army
Approved for public release; distribution unlimited

For more information on this publication, visit www.rand.org/t/RR1583

Library of Congress Control Number: 2018939056

ISBN: 978-0-8330-9985-3

Published by the RAND Corporation, Santa Monica, Calif.

Preface

In the project, "Assessing Army Leader Development in Professional Military Education," the U.S. Army Training and Doctrine Command, Combined Arms Center, asked the RAND Arroyo Center to conduct a study to support the Army's goals of developing leaders who can think critically and thrive under conditions of uncertainty. This report presents a review of the research literature that can provide a foundation for future study efforts addressing leader development. This review addresses the degree to which leader characteristics associated with attributes in the Army Leader Requirements Model can be developed through training and education and identifies approaches to measure those characteristics. Many of the findings from this review are relevant not only to leadership and to the Army but to personnel in a wide range of positions and organizations.

RAND operates under a "Federal-Wide Assurance" (FWA00003425) and complies with the Code of Federal Regulations for the Protection of Human Subjects Under United States Law (45 CFR 46), also known as "the Common Rule," as well as with the implementation guidance set forth in DoD Instruction 3216.02. As applicable, this compliance includes reviews and approvals by RAND's Institutional Review Board (the Human Subjects Protection Committee) and by the U.S. Army. The views of sources utilized in this study are solely their own and do not represent the official policy or position of DoD or the U.S. Government.

The research documented in this report was sponsored by the U.S. Army Training and Doctrine Command, Combined Arms Center, and was conducted within the RAND Arroyo Center's Personnel, Training, and Health Program. RAND Arroyo Center, part of the RAND Corporation, is a federally funded research and development center sponsored by the United States Army.

RAND's publications do not necessarily reflect the opinions of its research clients and sponsors.

The Project Unique Identification Code (PUIC) for the project that produced this document is RAN157322.

Contents

Figures

Tables

Summary

Complexity and uncertainty define the operational environment of today's U.S. Army. Army leaders face a myriad of challenges that demand a wide range of knowledge, skills, abilities, and other characteristics (KSAOs). Army Doctrine Reference Publication (ADRP) 6-22, *Army Leadership*, presents the Army Leader Requirements Model (ALRM), which specifies the attributes that leaders should possess and the core competencies they should demonstrate to meet these challenges (Headquarters, Department of the Army, 2012b). This report focuses on leader attributes. Attributes reflect KSAOs, which the ALRM groups into three categories: *intellect*, *presence*, and *character*.

To assist Army leadership development and training efforts, researchers from the RAND Arroyo Center conducted a literature review to answer two questions related to the ALRM attributes:

- To what degree can Army leadership attributes be taught?
- How can Army leadership attributes be measured?

In addition to answering these questions, the study team developed several recommendations to support the Army's ongoing efforts to assess the effectiveness of leader training and education.

Approach

Many of the ALRM attributes encompass a range of overlapping skills or behaviors. To answer the study questions, the study team drew upon more-narrowly defined *psychological constructs* associated with intellect, presence, and character that are well represented in theoretical and empirical research. The team reviewed research findings regarding the degree to which each construct is malleable, and, if malleable, the extent to which the construct can be developed through training and education. Alternatively, when relevant, the team addressed whether development can occur through work experience or is more normative in nature. In the third step, the team reviewed measures that are commonly used in research and practice to assess constructs associated with ALRM attributes.

Research Findings

Intellect

The ALRM defines *intellect* as the mental resources or tendencies that shape a leader's conceptual abilities and effectiveness. The ALRM identifies five specific attributes: mental agility, sound judgment, innovation, interpersonal tact, and expertise. Table S.1 displays constructs associated with intellect attributes.

The constructs vary in terms of malleability. With respect to general mental ability (GMA), research indicates that *crystallized intelligence*—abilities associated with general experience, depth of vocabulary, and verbal comprehension—is amenable to change through education and experience, but development is gradual. On the other hand, development of *fluid intelligence*—abilities that are most associated with working memory, abstract reasoning, attention, and processing new information—is largely normative in nature; it tends to peak in young adulthood and then decline gradually and monotonically through the remainder of life. Research on other constructs associated with intellect indicates that *domain-specific critical thinking (CT) skills*, *creative problem-solving*, and *expertise* can be improved through training and education.

The constructs related to intellect are typically measured with forced-choice tests, constructed-response (open-ended) tests, work sample tests, surveys, and in some cases, with interviews.

Table S.1
ALRM Attributes and Constructs Corresponding to Intellect

Attribute	Corresponding Constructs
Mental agility	General mental ability (GMA), critical thinking (CT), metacognition, creative problem-solving
Sound judgment	GMA, CT, metacognition, expertise
Innovation	Creative problem-solving
Interpersonal tact	Emotional intelligence (EI)
Expertise	Expertise

Table S.2 summarizes the research on the malleability of those constructs related to intellect in the Army ALRM and presents commonly used types of measures, as well as examples of specific measures, for each construct. A more comprehensive set of specific measures is provided in the main body of the report.

Presence

In the ALRM, *presence* refers to how others perceive leaders in terms of outward appearance and behavior. According to the ALRM, a leader's presence can inspire followers to do their best. This review addresses three constructs related to presence, shown in Table S.3.

Constructs related to presence can be developed and/or enhanced over time through training and other means. *Physical fitness* and *resilience* are most amenable to improvement through training and education. *Generalized self-efficacy* increases through repeated successes in different situations; thus, it may change indirectly through successes in training and education, but over long periods of time. Longitudinal research shows that the social dominance facets of *extraversion* change across the lifespan, but research suggests that such change occurs in response to shifts in role demands and expectations. This suggests that social dominance is not amenable to change through training and education but might be developed through job assignments.

Constructs related to presence are typically measured using tests and surveys.

Table S.2
Summary of Malleability and Measures: Intellect

Construct	Malleability	Measures
GMA	Evidence suggests that crystallized intelligence can be enhanced, whereas fluid intelligence peaks in the mid-twenties and declines gradually over time, with the possible exception of working memory, which does not decline or can be enhanced.	• Standardized, forced-choice (multiple-choice) tests such as the Armed Services Vocational Aptitude Battery
CT	Strong evidence exists for positive effects of training on CT skills, particularly when domain-specific; there is less (although positive) evidence for effects of training on dispositional aspects of CT.	• Standardized, forced-choice commercial tests of domain-general critical thinking skills, such as the Watson-Glaser Critical Thinking Appraisal (Watson and Glaser, 1980) • Constructed-response (open-ended) tests, such as the Halpern Critical Thinking Assessment (which also includes forced-choice items) (Halpern, 2010) • Self-report surveys of dispositional aspects of critical thinking, such as the Actively Open-Minded Thinking Scale (Stanovich and West, 1998)
Metacognition	There is little research regarding the trainability of metacognitive skills outside of academic contexts.	• Self-report surveys, such as the Metacognitive Awareness Inventory (Schraw and Dennison, 1994)
Creative problem solving	Strong evidence exists regarding positive effects of creativity training across diverse populations. Dispositional aspects of creativity increase in young adulthood, but the cause of these changes is not well understood.	• Constructed-response tests, such as the Alternate Uses Test (Wallach and Kogan, 1965) • Self-report surveys of behaviors or biographic information such as the Biographical Inventory of Creative Behaviors (Batey, 2007) • Self-report dispositional scales from surveys measuring the Big Five personality factor of openness to experience, such as the Tailored Adaptive Personality Assessment System (TAPAS) (Stark et al., 2014) and the International Personality Item Pool (IPIP) (Goldberg, 1999)

Table S.2—Continued

Construct	Malleability	Measures
Emotional intelligence (EI)	There is a lack of robust research on the effectiveness of interventions intended to develop EI.	• Multiple-choice commercial tests such as the Mayer-Salovey-Caruso Emotional Intelligence Test (Mayer, Salovey, Caruso, and Sitarenios, 2003) • Self-report surveys, such as the Wong and Law Emotional Intelligence Scale (Wong and Law, 2002)
Expertise	Expertise develops through job experience, training, and education. Deliberate practice is a critical factor contributing to becoming an expert in a particular domain.	• Situational judgment tests (SJTs), such as the Tacit Knowledge for Military Leaders test (Hedlund et al., 2003) • Customized written tests, work sample tests, SJTs, and interviews

Table S.3
ALRM Attributes and Constructs Corresponding to Presence

Attribute	Corresponding Constructs
Military and professional bearing	Physical fitness, EI
Fitness	Physical fitness
Confidence	Generalized self-efficacy, extraversion, EI
Resilience	Resilience

Table S.4 summarizes the research on the malleability of those constructs related to presence in the Army ALRM and presents commonly used types of measures, along with specific examples, for each construct. A more comprehensive set of specific measures is provided in the main body of the report.

Character

Army doctrine defines *character* as the set of an individual's morals and ethics; character helps leaders distinguish right from wrong and to make the right choices in difficult situations (Headquarters, Department of the Army, 2012b). Constructs from the research literature related to character are presented in Table S.5.

Table S.4
Summary of Malleability and Measures: Presence

Construct	Malleability	Measures
Physical fitness	Physical fitness is highly malleable, particularly with appropriate physical training programs.	• Tests of physical performance, such as the Army Physical Fitness Test • Self-report surveys of dispositional aspects of physical fitness, such as the physical conditioning scale of the TAPAS (Stark et al., 2014)
Generalized self-efficacy (GSE)	GSE is considered a dynamic (rather than static) personality trait that is somewhat malleable and will increase over time and with successful experiences in different domains; therefore, training may have an indirect effect on development of GSE.	• Self-report surveys such as the New Generalized Self-Efficacy scale (Chen, Gully, and Eden, 2001)
Extraversion	Studies of personality traits across the lifespan show increases in social dominance facets of extraversion up to age 40; these changes are thought to occur in response to shifts in role expectations, suggesting that training will not have direct effects on extraversion.	• Self-report dispositional scales from surveys measuring the Big Five personality factor of extraversion, such as the TAPAS (Stark et al., 2014) and the IPIP (Goldberg, 1999)
Resilience	Studies of resiliency training programs show that resilience can be developed or enhanced.	• Self-report surveys such as the Dispositional Resilience Scale (Bartone, 1995)

There is limited research or consensus about the malleability of constructs associated with character. Research findings on changes in *ethical decisionmaking* are mixed, and there is insufficient literature to draw conclusions about development of *initiative. Conscientiousness* changes across the lifespan, but such changes are thought to occur as a result of shifts in role demands and expectations (e.g., pursuing a career and leading a family). *Motivation to lead* also appears to change through job experiences as well as social learning, but would not be expected to be developed directly via training and education.

Table S.5
ALRM Attributes and Constructs Corresponding to Character

Attribute	Corresponding Constructs
Army values	Ethical decisionmaking, conscientiousness, initiative
Empathy	EI
Discipline	Conscientiousness
Warrior ethos and service ethos	Motivation to lead, affective commitment

Likewise, the content of training and education is unlikely to directly influence *affective commitment*, which is considered a job attitude influenced by organizational practices such as role clarification and fair treatment, although opportunities for training and education might influence this construct.

Common measures of constructs related to presence include self-report surveys, "other reports" in which coworkers or supervisors rate the target individual, SJTs, and interviews.

Table S.6 summarizes the research on the malleability of those constructs related to character in the Army ALRM and presents commonly used types of measures, along with examples, for each construct. A more comprehensive set of specific measures is provided in the main body of the report.

To What Degree Can Army Leadership Attributes Be Taught?

Based on our review of the literature, we summarize the degree to which each psychological construct associated with ALRM attributes can be developed through training and education by displaying them along a continuum ranging from less to more malleable (see Figure S.1). We supplement this figure by identifying attributes that may be malleable through other means, such as work experiences or organizational practices, and highlighting attributes for which additional research is needed to draw conclusions about malleability.

Table S.6
Summary of Malleability and Measures: Character

Construct	Malleability	Measures
Ethical decisionmaking	Research findings conflict about development of ethical decisionmaking through training. It is likely that program characteristics affect the impact of training.	• Situation judgments tests, such as the Defining Issues Test-2 (Rest, Narvaez, Bebeau, and Thoma, 1999) • Self-report surveys, such as the Ethical Leadership Scale (Brown, Treviño, and Harrison, 2005)
Initiative	There is insufficient empirical literature to draw strong conclusions about the trainability of initiative.	• SJTs, such as Bledow and Frese (2009) • Self-report surveys of dispositional aspects of initiative, such as the Proactive Personality scale (Bateman and Crant, 1993) • Other-report surveys, such as the measure of Extra-role Behaviors (Van Dyne and LePine, 1998) • Interviews of personal initiative (Frese et al., 1997)
Conscientiousness	Formal training and education is unlikely to have a direct effect on conscientiousness. Changes in conscientiousness across the lifespan are thought to occur in response to shifting role demands and expectations, suggesting that job experiences might affect conscientiousness.	• Self-report dispositional scales from surveys measuring the Big Five personality factor of conscientiousness, such as the TAPAS (Stark et al., 2014) and the IPIP (Goldberg, 1999)
Motivation to lead	Formal training and education are unlikely to have a direct effect on motivation to lead, but some findings indicate that it can be developed through social learning and job experiences.	• Self-report surveys such as the Motivation to Lead scale (Chan and Drasgow, 2001)
Affective commitment	Affective commitment is considered a job attitude that is influenced by organizational practices, such as clarifying individual roles and perceptions of fair treatment. Training and education content are unlikely to have a direct effect on affective commitment.	• Self-report surveys such as the Affective Commitment Questionnaire (Allen and Meyer, 1990; Meyer, Allen, and Smith, 1993)

Figure S.1
Degree of Malleability of ALRM Constructs

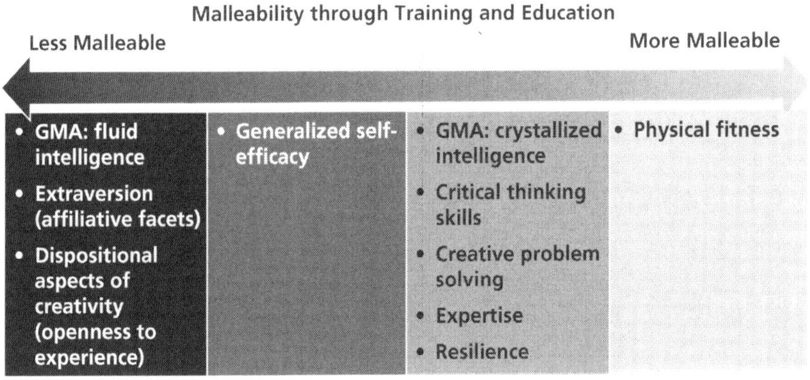

Constructs that may be malleable through work experiences or organizational practices

- Conscientiousness
- Extraversion (social dominance facets)
- Affective commitment

Insufficient research evidence regarding malleability

- Dispositional aspects of critical thinking
- Metacognition
- Emotional intelligence
- Ethical decisionmaking
- Initiative
- Motivation to lead

SOURCE: Adapted from Mueller-Hanson et al., 2005.
RAND *RR1583-S.1*

Recommendations

Assess return on investment of training and education programs. This review indicates that constructs relevant to Army leadership range in their degree of malleability. For example, GMA is unlikely to be modified through training and education, whereas physical fitness is much more malleable. Other constructs, such as CT skills, creative problem-solving, and expertise, can be developed through training, but development may be gradual. Still other constructs (e.g., conscientiousness) are unlikely to change through training but might be developed through job assignments. Thus, a critical question for the Army is to determine whether the return on investment is greater for training and development interventions compared to selection and placement strategies.

When investigating whether training and education bring about changes in leader characteristics, there are a number of methodological and practical considerations pertaining to selection of measures and design of evaluation programs.

Consider scalability and cost-effectiveness when selecting measures. The measures reviewed in the report comprise a range of approaches. The predominant approaches include forced-choice tests, constructed-response tests, work sample tests, surveys, and interviews, each of which has different advantages and disadvantages.

- Forced-choice (i.e., multiple-choice) tests and surveys can be used to assess a range of constructs. These instruments can be scored efficiently, making them highly scalable and cost effective for large groups. The study team recommends use of forced-choice measures where possible.
- Constructed-response (open-ended) tests may produce better assessments of complex knowledge and skills and better reflect tasks in actual job settings but typically take longer to administer and, therefore, impose greater response burden, are more labor intensive and costly to score, and require human judges who are trained to provide reliable and valid ratings.
- Work sample tests are particularly good for assessing complex or less tangible knowledge and skills but can be costly to develop, often require one-on-one administration, and may require trained human judges to score responses.
- Interviews require one-on-one administration and involve subjective judgment, which is prone to biases. Use of structured interviews can improve reliability and validity compared to unstructured interviews, but the team recommends using reliable and valid self-report instruments rather than interviews to assess constructs related to the ALRM.

Let the topic of study and relevant theory guide the content of measures. The constructs that are potentially relevant in studies of leader attributes and competencies are often too numerous to measure. To limit response burden, evaluation efforts should use measures that correspond directly to the topic under investigation (e.g., if evaluating the effects of training to improve CT, relevant measures would include assessments of CT skills and dispositions). Theory and past research can guide selection of potential correlates to measure (for CT skills, these might include GMA and metacognition). Including such measures can help determine the degree to which the outcome can be explained by training and education or by other factors.

Design evaluations to rule out threats to validity. When assessing the extent to which training and education interventions lead to improvement in constructs, the study design determines the kinds of conclusions one can draw. Comparing an intervention group (pretest, training intervention, posttest) with a control group (pretest and posttest only) can rule out many threats to internal validity, i.e., factors that prevent the researcher from drawing conclusions about the effects of the intervention. Random assignment of participants to groups helps to ensure that changes in knowledge or skills occurred because of the intervention as opposed to resulting from differences in characteristics of the participants in each group.

Administer or collect measures of some constructs for officers on a routine basis. GMA and three of the Big Five personality factors—openness to experience, conscientiousness, and extraversion—are related to many of the ALRM attributes. Whereas Army enlisted personnel complete assessments of GMA and the Big Five factors during recruitment, the Army does not systematically collect such measures for officers. Obtaining measures of these constructs for prospective Army leaders prior to or upon commissioning could prove useful for job placement and for use in ongoing Army research (e.g., to understand the effects of training and a range of other interventions or topics of interest). Finally, baseline measures of GMA and the Big Five, coupled with reassessments over time, can help the Army understand how training and experience influence key cognitive abilities and personality characteristics.

Future Directions

There are several constructs with more limited research or a lack of established measures that are related to ALRM attributes and merit further consideration. These include *cognitive flexibility*, *adaptive expertise*, and *frame-switching capabilities*, which are relevant to mental agility, and *social intelligence*, which is relevant to interpersonal tact. Other constructs associated with leader effectiveness but not identified explicitly in the ALRM include *adaptability* and *systems thinking*. Research on leadership should also consider situational factors, such as task characteristics, which can affect the association of leader attributes and performance, and organizational culture, which can influence the development and expression of leader attributes. In addition to considering other constructs, there are other measures that may be suitable for the assessment of ALRM attributes.

This review focused on development of attributes in leaders, but leaders also play an important role in developing many of these attributes in others. Thus, leader training and education should address which attributes are more or less malleable and, for attributes that can be changed, provide strategies for developing these attributes in others. In addition, whereas this report focuses on ALRM attributes, a comprehensive review of leader competencies could prove fruitful. Taken together, these efforts can enhance the Army's understanding of the factors that contribute to effective leadership and can guide leader development and selection practices.

Acknowledgments

We wish to acknowledge our RAND colleagues, Louay Constant, Bryan Hallmark, Kun Yuan, Andrew Naber, Katya Migacheva, and Michael Shanley for their intellectual contributions to this effort. We are grateful to Sean Robson and Stephen Zaccaro for their comprehensive and insightful reviews of this report. Many thanks to Michael Hansen for his ongoing support and guidance on this project. We thank Barbara Hennessey, Laura Pavlock-Albright, Patricia McGarry, Julie Ann Tajiri, and Laura Coley for their help in preparing this document.

CHAPTER ONE

Introduction

Today's military full-spectrum operating environment is demanding and complex. Army leaders thus face a myriad of challenges that demand a wide range of knowledge, skills, abilities, and other characteristics (KSAOs). The Army Leader Requirements Model (ALRM) (see Headquarters, Department of the Army, 2012b, which is Army Doctrine Reference Publication [ADRP] 6-22) delineates the attributes that leaders should possess and the core competencies they should demonstrate to meet these challenges. As illustrated in Figure 1.1, attributes reflect KSAOs, which the ALRM groups into three categories: *character*, *presence*, and *intellect*. Competencies reflect the behaviors that leaders are expected to demonstrate on the job. ADRP 6-22 groups these competencies into three categories: *lead*, *develop*, and *achieve*.[1]

Many of these attributes and competencies are also reflected in the Army Human Dimension Strategy for 2015 (U.S. Department of the Army, 2015). Like the ALRM, the Human Dimension Strategy posits a number of psychological constructs integral to the success of future Army leaders at all levels of command.

This study supports leadership training efforts of the Army Training and Doctrine Command, Combined Arms Center, by examining the required leader attributes as specified in the ALRM. We focus on attributes, rather than competencies, because attributes reflect characteristics of individuals that may be amenable to change and, as suggested by the ALRM, are the starting point to bringing about core leader

[1] To elaborate, these competencies are *lead* others; *develop* the environment, themselves, others, and the profession as a whole; and *achieve* organizational goals.

Figure 1.1
The Army Leader Requirements Model (ALRM)

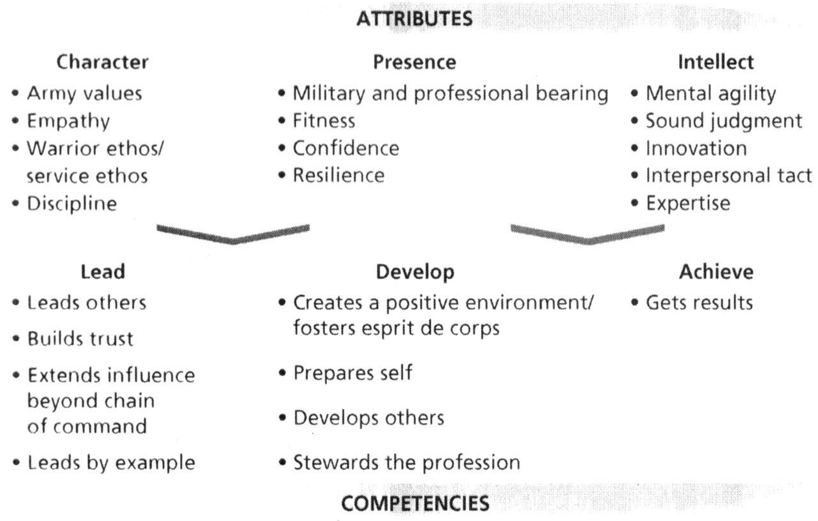

SOURCE: Headquarters, Department of the Army, 2012b.
RAND RR1583-1.1

competencies. However, while the attributes associated with *character*, *presence*, and *intellect* are important aspects of leadership, the attributes in the ALRM are not necessarily the terms or concepts found in the theoretical or empirical literature. To understand the degree to which attributes in these categories can be taught and measured, we mapped the ALRM attributes onto psychological constructs that are most commonly reported in the literature, as evidenced by being the subject of meta-analyses, comprehensive reviews, or numerous primary studies. Findings can be used to inform ongoing and future development of Army education programs and learning objectives.

Research Questions and Study Approach

This report brings together multiple strands of research to answer two questions pertaining to Army leader training and education. The first question asks: ***To what degree can Army leadership attributes be taught?*** To answer this question, we work toward identifying the degree to which constructs associated with leader attributes are relatively fixed or malleable. The constructs we investigate can be arrayed on a continuum consisting of states at one end and traits at the other (e.g., Luthans and Youssef, 2007). A state can be momentary and very changeable (e.g., feelings or moods, like pleasure or happiness), whereas a trait is very stable and difficult to change (e.g., heritable characteristics, some cognitive abilities). Constructs occupying intermediate positions on the continuum are malleable to varying degrees.

The degree of malleability is important because it has implications for human resource management. Personnel selection practices, such as the use of tests and other assessment instruments, are appropriate for identifying whether personnel possess attributes that are relatively fixed (i.e., trait or trait-like). Personnel development activities, i.e., training and education, may be appropriate for attributes that are malleable, but this will depend on how changes in the attributes typically occur. For example, change in some attributes tends to be normative in that most people experience the same kinds of changes at particular points in life, which are likely brought about by genetic factors or experiences that occur at particular ages for most people (Roberts, Walton, and Viechtbauer, 2006). If such changes arise primarily from genetic factors or occur in childhood or later in life (among the elderly), then the Army can do little to affect development of such attributes. In contrast, evidence indicating that attributes are malleable via training and education suggests that the Army can have a much greater influence on attribute development. While the focus of this review is bringing about change through training and education, we note where the Army might be able to develop leader attributes through job experiences or assignments.

In past research, Mueller-Hanson et al. (2005) rated the trainability of a range of KSAOs associated with adaptability. Mueller-Hanson et al. concluded that cognitive ability, openness to experience, resiliency, tolerance for ambiguity, and achievement motivation are considered to be resistant to change (i.e., they are traits or trait-like), whereas domain-specific knowledge and adaptive experience in varied settings should be readily modifiable with training (i.e., they are states, or state-like). The authors concluded that problem-solving/decisionmaking, metacognitive skills, general self-efficacy, communication skills, and self- and situation awareness are amenable to change to varied degrees, although much effort is needed to bring about significant improvements. Our report addresses many of these constructs as well as other characteristics relevant to the ALRM. We also review more recent research findings, which lead us to draw different conclusions about the malleability of some constructs important for leader effectiveness.

The second question we address in the report is: ***How can Army leadership attributes be measured?*** To answer this, we review existing measures of constructs associated with ALRM attributes. Identifying measures is needed to support selecting personnel for jobs and determining whether personnel develop attributes in training or through job experiences. Assessing these attributes is also important to evaluate the effectiveness of personnel practices. For example, the appropriateness of using a particular test to measure an attribute is assessed, in part, by analyzing the association of scores on the test with subsequent job performance. We focus on measures that are prevalent in research and practice and that have evidence of acceptable reliability and validity.[2]

---

[2] Reliability refers to consistency or reproducibility of measurement. Assessment of reliability uses correlational methods and depends, in part, on the type of measure being used. For example, *coefficient alpha*, or *internal consistency reliability*, indicates whether respondents give similar answers to similar types of questions (e.g., multiple-choice questions on a test or items on a scale measuring a particular concept). *Test-retest reliability* indicates if respondents give similar answers to the same questions over time. *Interrater-reliability* is used when raters make subjective judgments of stimuli (e.g., responses to interview questions, creativity of solutions to problems); it indicates whether different raters provide similar ratings of the same stimuli.

Validity refers to whether a measure assesses what it intends or purports to measure. Common sources of validity include face validity, content validity, construct validity, criterion-related validity, and discriminant validity. Face validity is assessed subjectively by respondents and reflects views of whether the measure assesses what it purports to measure. Content validity reflects the degree to which a measure assesses all relevant facets of a construct; it tends to be assessed using qualitative methods. Construct validity is typically assessed by calculating the correlation of scores on a particular measure with scores on other measures that purport to measure the same construct (for example, a significant, positive correlation of scores on a new test of critical thinking skills and scores on other tests of critical thinking [CT] skills would provide construct validity for the new test). Criterion-related validity assesses whether measures are associated with outcomes; for example, a significant, positive correlation of general

However, we present only a sample of the many measures that may be available for some constructs discussed in this review. Unless noted, the measures we discuss are in the public domain and are free to use.

In reviewing measures, we focus largely on self-report methods, i.e., tests (to assess knowledge or skills) and surveys (to assess attitudes or dispositions). Written or computerized tests and surveys using forced-choice (i.e., multiple choice) questions are advantageous in that they provide objective measures (i.e., quantitative data, and in the case of tests, right or wrong answers) and can be administered and scored using automated methods. In contrast, tests or surveys using constructed-response (open-ended) questions are much more labor intensive and costly to score and typically take longer to administer and, therefore, are not readily scalable for large groups. For some constructs, we discuss other approaches to measurement, such as work sample tests and interviews, where appropriate. We present a more comprehensive summary of the advantages and disadvantages of different approaches to measurement in the concluding chapter of this report.

Measuring ALRM attributes poses a challenge, as most are multidimensional in nature; that is, they encompass a range of overlapping skills or behaviors. To answer our study questions, we draw upon more narrowly defined constructs (i.e., psychological concepts or variables) that are well represented in theoretical and empirical research. In some instances, there were relevant constructs that we opted not to include because they lacked a sufficient body of research. We discuss these constructs as avenues for future research in Chapter Five.

Tables 1.1 to 1.3 present the constructs we address for each attribute category (intellect, character, and presence). In the first column of each table, we present the attributes; in the second column, we present how the attributes are defined in the ALRM; and in the third column, we identify the constructs that correspond to attributes.

---

mental ability and CT test scores may provide evidence that general mental ability is a valid predictor of CT skills. Discriminant validity reflects whether measures of different constructs are, in fact, unrelated (not correlated with each other). Our selection of measures was based largely on construct, criterion-related, and/or discriminant validity. For more background on types of validity, see Allen and Yen (1979).

Table 1.1
Intellect Attributes, Definitions, and Corresponding Psychological Constructs

Attribute	ALRM Definition	Corresponding Constructs
Mental agility	• Flexibility of mind; the ability to break habitual thought patterns • Anticipating or adapting to uncertain or changing situations; to think through outcomes when current decisions or actions are not producing desired effects • The ability to apply multiple perspectives and approaches	• General mental ability (GMA)* • Critical thinking (CT)* • Metacognition* • Creative problem-solving*
Sound judgment	• The capacity to assess situations shrewdly and draw sound conclusions • The tendency to form sound opinions, make sensible decisions and reliable guesses • The ability to assess strengths and weaknesses of subordinates, peers, and the enemy to create appropriate solutions and action	• GMA* • CT* • Metacognition* • Expertise
Innovation	• The ability to introduce new ideas based on opportunity or challenging circumstances • Creativity in producing ideas and objects that are both novel and appropriate	• Creative problem-solving*
Interpersonal tact	• The capacity to understand interactions with others • Being aware of how others see you and sensing how to interact with them effectively • Being conscious of character, reactions, and motives of self and others and how they affect interactions • Recognizing diversity and displaying self-control, balance, and stability	• Emotional intelligence**
Expertise	• Possessing facts, beliefs, logical assumptions, and understanding in relevant areas	• Expertise

SOURCE: The attributes and definitions above are from Headquarters, Department of the Army, 2012b, Table 5-1 ("Summary of the attributes associated with *Intellect*").

NOTE: Some of the constructs are associated with multiple attributes within an attribute category (denoted by *) or with multiple attributes across attribute categories (denoted by **).

Organization of This Report

Chapters Two to Four present the three attribute categories, intellect, presence, and character, in turn. For each category, we discuss the constructs associated with the attributes shown in Tables 1.1 to 1.3. Each chapter is organized in four parts:

First, we define the construct.

Second, we briefly summarize research findings about the association of the construct with leader performance (where available), followed by a summary of findings about the association of the construct with job performance more generally. In the absence of studies examining job performance, we report results from research on outcomes associated with performance or organizational success, such as scholastic achievement, situational awareness, goal attainment, employee turnover, or other behaviors that contribute to the good of the organization (contextual performance). We rely largely on meta-analyses and comprehensive reviews if available; otherwise, we discuss specific studies.[3]

Third, we review empirical research on the malleability of the construct, focusing on research addressing changes in adulthood. If malleable, we also discuss available evidence regarding factors contributing to the potential for change. Although we focus on development via formal training and education, we also note attributes that can change through work experience (such as changes in roles) or whether attribute development is more normative in nature (changes tend to occur at specific stages in life).

Fourth, we present specific measures of the construct, or in the absence of specific measures, we describe measurement approaches.

At the end of each chapter, we summarize the evidence of malleability of the relevant constructs through training and education and work experience (where relevant) along with a list of construct measures.

---

[3] Meta-analysis is a statistical technique that combines results across independent studies of similar topics. Results of meta-analyses are often based on thousands of observations and can provide substantial statistical power to estimate effects.

Table 1.2
Presence Attributes, Definitions, and Corresponding Psychological Constructs

Attribute	ALRM Definition	Corresponding Constructs
Military and professional bearing	• Possessing a commanding presence • Projecting a professional image of authority; displaying fitness, courtesy, and proper military appearance[a]	• Physical fitness* • Emotional intelligence**
Fitness	• Having sound health, strength, and endurance that support one's emotional health and conceptual abilities under prolonged stress	• Physical fitness*[b]
Confidence	• Projecting self-confidence and certainty in the unit's ability to succeed in its missions • Demonstrating composure and outward calm through control over one's emotions	• Generalized self-efficacy* • Extraversion • Emotional intelligence**
Resilience	• Showing a tendency to recover quickly from setbacks, shock, injuries, adversity, and stress while maintaining a mission and organizational focus	• Resilience

SOURCE: The attributes and definitions are from Headquarters, Department of the Army, 2012b, Table 4-1 ("Summary of the attributes associated with *Presence*").

NOTE: Some of the constructs are associated with multiple attributes within an attribute category (denoted by *) or with multiple attributes across attribute categories (denoted by **).

[a] In the ALRM, physical fitness is identified as an aspect of military and professional bearing and as a separate attribute. "Courtesy" is not clearly defined in the ALRM, but perhaps maps on to aspects of emotional intelligence, which we include here. In future iterations of the ALRM, providing a more concrete definition of military and professional bearing could facilitate efforts to develop and measure this attribute. Because proper military appearance is not a psychological construct, we do not discuss it in this review.

[b] Given the ADRP 6-22 definition of fitness, a range of topics, including nutrition, sleep, physical health, psychological health, and spirituality, could be reviewed, but these constructs are outside the scope of this project.

In Chapter Five, we summarize key findings regarding malleability of leader attributes and discuss strategies to determine whether to emphasize training and development or selection for these attributes. We then present additional topics related to measurement, describe methods for studying the effects of training and education on develop-

Table 1.3
Character Attributes, Definitions, and Corresponding Psychological Constructs

Attribute	ALRM Definition	Corresponding Constructs
Army values	• Values are principles, standards, or qualities considered essential for successful leaders • Values are fundamental to help people discern right from wrong in any situation • The Army has seven values to develop in all Army individuals: loyalty, duty, respect, selfless service, honor, integrity, and personal courage	• Ethical decisionmaking • Conscientiousness* • Initiative
Empathy	• The propensity to experience something from another person's point of view • The ability to identify with and enter into another person's feelings and emotions • The desire to care for and take care of soldiers and others	• Emotional intelligence**
Discipline	• Control of one's own behavior according to Army values; mindset to obey and enforce good orderly practices in administrative, organizational, training, and operational duties	• Conscientiousness*
Warrior ethos/ service ethos	• The internal shared attitudes and beliefs that embody the spirit of the Army profession for soldiers and Army civilians alike, reflecting a commitment to the nation, mission, unit, and fellow soldiers	• Motivation to lead • Affective commitment

SOURCE: The attributes and definitions are from Headquarters, Department of the Army, 2012b, Table 3-1 ("Summary of the attributes associated with *Character*").

NOTE: Some of the constructs are associated with multiple attributes within an attribute category (denoted by *) or with multiple attributes across attribute categories (denoted by **).

ment of leader attributes, and provide recommendations regarding routine assessment of leader attributes. We conclude by noting the limitations of our review and proposing additional leader attributes and related topics to address in future research.

CHAPTER TWO

Intellect Attributes

The complexity inherent to the duties of modern military leaders demands heavy reliance on intellect. ADRP 6-22 defines *intellect* as the mental resources or tendencies that shape a leader's conceptual abilities and effectiveness and identifies five specific intellect attributes: mental agility, sound judgment, innovation, interpersonal tact, and expertise. In this chapter, we review related constructs from theoretical and empirical research that correspond with intellect attributes. These constructs include general mental ability (GMA), critical thinking (CT), metacognition, creative problem-solving, emotional intelligence, and expertise.

This chapter is organized according to those constructs. First, we define the construct and then summarize research findings about the association of the construct with leader performance (if available), followed by general job performance or related outcomes. We then review empirical research on the malleability of the construct. Finally, we present specific measures of the construct. We summarize key findings in Table 2.7 at the end of this chapter.

General Mental Ability

Definition

Gottfredson's (1997) definition of intelligence, GMA, reflects views of scholars from a wide spectrum of disciplines and perspectives. She defines intelligence as:

> a very general mental capacity that, among other things, involves the ability to reason, plan, solve problems, think abstractly, comprehend complex ideas, learn quickly, and learn from experience. It is not merely book learning, a narrow academic skill, or test-taking smarts. Rather, it reflects a broader and deeper capability for comprehending our surroundings—"catching on," "making sense" of things, or "figuring out" what to do (p. 13).

Indeed, there are numerous specific cognitive abilities (e.g., verbal, quantitative, spatial, and reasoning) and many theories of intelligence (e.g., Cattell, 1971; Gardner, 1993; Guilford, 1967; Sternberg, 1985). However, many scholars argue that these specific abilities share a common thread: GMA.[1]

Association with Performance

Since Spearman's influential (1904) article "General Intelligence, Objectively Determined and Measured," numerous studies have examined the association of GMA with various indicators of leadership performance. Meta-analyses suggest the strength of this relationship range from moderately weak (Bass, 2008; Judge, Colbert, and Ilies, 2004) to somewhat strong (Lord, De Vader, and Alliger, 1986). Research has also found support for this relationship in longitudinal studies conducted for the Army. For example, Bartone, Snook, and Tremble (2002) found that cognitive ability predicted leader performance in a study tracking a cohort of cadets across all four years at the U.S. Military Academy.

GMA is a moderate to strong predictor of job performance more generally, which has been replicated in U.S. samples (Hunter and Hunter, 1984; Judge et al., 1999; Schmidt, 2002; Schmidt and Hunter, 2004) and European samples (Salgado et al., 2006). We note, however, that job complexity affects the strength of the GMA-job performance relationship such that jobs with higher complexity yield stronger relationships between GMA and performance than jobs with lower

[1] This topic is somewhat controversial, however, as other scholars argue that evidence does not support the concept of a general mental ability as a common factor underlying other intelligences (e.g., see Horn and Masunaga, 2006; Salthouse, 2012).

complexity (Ones et al., 2010). Given the complexity of being an Army leader, we expect that GMA plays an important role in leader performance.

Malleability

The malleability of GMA has long been debated. Evidence indicates that GMA is due largely to hereditary factors (Plomin and DeFries, 1998; Shakeshaft et al., 2015); however, the environment also plays a role (e.g., Flynn, 1987). Many researchers have viewed intelligence as mostly fixed (Jensen, 1998); however, others have argued for its malleability (Feuerstein, 1980). While intelligence levels are rather resistant to *relative* change (i.e., one's intelligence capabilities relative to other people), a positive change is possible and expected within an individual over a lifetime (Salthouse, 2012) as well as through training (Buschkuehl and Jaeggi, 2010; Jaeggi, Buschkuehl, Jonides, and Perrig, 2008; Sternberg, 2008).

From a normative developmental perspective, empirical research on mental ability across the lifetime frequently differentiates between crystallized intelligence and fluid intelligence.[2] *Crystallized intelligence* represents abilities that are most associated with general experience, depth of vocabulary, and verbal comprehension (Cattell, 1971). Over the course of one's career, individuals amass a wealth of knowledge, and research suggests this accumulation continues until approximately 60 to 70 years of age and then gradually declines (Horn and Masunaga, 2006; Salthouse, 2012). *Fluid intelligence* refers to the abilities that are most associated with working memory, abstract reasoning, attention, and processing new information (Cattell, 1971). Across different samples, methods, and measures, cognitive psychologists consistently conclude that fluid intelligence peaks in the mid-20s and then demonstrates a gradual and monotonic decline through the remainder of life (Salthouse, 2012; see also Horn and Masunaga, 2006). Some researchers have found fluid intelligence to be very similar to GMA (Gustafsson, 2002;

---

[2] Fluid and crystallized intelligence correlate strongly (approximately 0.70) (Gustafsson, 2002).

Carroll, 1993) or suggest that fluid intelligence and GMA are one and the same (Kvist and Gustafsson, 2008).

From a training perspective, crystallized intelligence is often considered amenable to change through formal education and/or experiential learning, although development factors, including educational opportunities and child-rearing practices that emphasize the value of formal education and knowledge acquisition, influence development of crystallized intelligence (Horn and Masunaga, 2006). The literature, however, still points to conflicting conclusions regarding the effects of training to improve fluid intelligence. Some studies conclude that training will not yield gains (e.g., Harrison et al., 2013) and others suggest training will prove valuable (e.g., Busckuehl and Jaeggi, 2010; Jaeggi et al., 2008; Sternberg, 2008). Much of this research targets working memory as a means for improving fluid intelligence. Working memory is typically viewed as the part of long-term memory that is available for active information processing, including the placement and retrieval of information into and out of storage. To examine the potential effects of training, Au et al. (2014) conducted a meta-analysis of 20 studies, including healthy participants between ages 18 and 50, and found a small but statistically significant positive effect of training on fluid intelligence.[3] In contrast, Sprenger et al. (2013) found that while certain aspects of working memory may improve because of training, these improvements did not generalize to other nonsimilar cognitive abilities or even to other, untrained aspects of working memory. Other evidence suggests there may be a dosage effect, with a greater duration and amount of training yielding larger and more enduring gains in fluid intelligence (Jaeggi et al., 2008; Jaeggi et al., 2014; Schmiedek, Lövdén, and Lindenberger, 2014). For example, Jaeggi et al. (2014) found significant improvement for study participants who had daily training sessions for 17 or 19 days but not for participants who had 8 or 12 training days (training sessions were approximately 25 minutes per day). Additionally, studies suggest

---

[3] This meta-analysis consisted of studies of *n*-back training conducted over one week or longer. In *n*-back training, trainees are presented with a series of stimuli (e.g., shapes or letters) and must decide if the current stimulus matches one presented *n* trials ago, where *n* is a number that can be adjusted to influence cognitive workload. The stimuli in *n*-back tasks can be presented different ways, e.g., visually and/or aurally.

that as people age, training is less effective for improving fluid intelligence (Sternberg et al., 2013). In light of continually emerging and conflicting findings, more research is needed on whether fluid intelligence can be improved through training.

Measurement Tools

There are hundreds of GMA measures available to scientists, individual practitioners, and organizations that span the spectrum of empirical support, ranging from tests developed with limited empirical research to tests developed for commercial use with decades of empirical research (Ones et al., 2010). For adult civilians, common measures of GMA include standardized tests for undergraduate and graduate admissions[4] (e.g., SAT, ACT, and Graduate Record Examination [GRE]) and other commercially available tests that measure global or specific abilities, such as the Wonderlic Personnel Test (Wonderlic, 2012), Wechsler Adult Intelligence Scale-IV (Wechsler, Coalson, and Raiford, 2008), Raven's Standard Progressive Matrices (Raven, Raven, and Court, 1998), the Nelson-Denny Reading Test (Brown, Fishco, and Hanna, 1993), and the Miller Analogies Test (MAT; see Pearson Assessment, 2016).[5]

To enlist in the armed services, prospective candidates are required to take the Armed Services Vocational Aptitude Battery (ASVAB). The ASVAB consists of a battery of standardized tests and also yields a composite score, known as the Armed Forces Qualification Test (AFQT), which combines ASVAB subsections of arithmetic reasoning, mathematics knowledge, and verbal expression. The ASVAB can be administered in both paper-and-pencil and computerized format. The ASVAB has been used as a predictor in numerous studies of military personnel; it predicts outcomes such as success in training, first-term attrition, and job performance in a range of occupations (e.g., Welsh, Kucinkas, and Curran, 1990). However, neither the ASVAB nor any other test of GMA

---

[4] Scholars differentiate between abilities and knowledge, and there are claims that tests such as the SAT and ACT measure knowledge more than ability (Salthouse, 2012). However, these tests have been shown to have strong correlations with measures of GMA (e.g., Frey and Detterman, 2004; Koenig, Frey, and Detterman, 2008) and are often used as indicators of GMA.

[5] Pearson Assessment, 2016.

is administered to commissioned officers in the Army on a systematic basis. We discuss the value of administering such tests in the concluding chapter of this report.

Critical Thinking Skills

Definition

ADRP 6-22 emphasizes CT as a component of mental agility. CT is related to, but distinct from, GMA (e.g., Klaczynski et al., 1997; Toplak and Stanovich, 2002; West, Toplak, and Stanovich, 2008). There is disagreement about how to define CT, but many scholars view CT as consisting of two components: skills or abilities, and dispositional characteristics (e.g., Halpern, 1998; Klacyznski et al., 1997; Stanovich and Stanovich, 2010). CT skills or abilities reflect cognitive activities such as reasoning, disjunctive thinking (i.e., considering all possible states of the world when responding to a problem; Toplak and Stanovich, 2002) and reflective thinking (e.g., judging the credibility of sources and quality of an argument; Ennis, 1993). Some researchers view CT skills as general, whereas others focus on CT in specific domains (e.g., Abrami et al., 2008; Toplak and Stanovich, 2002). Dispositional factors associated with CT typically reflect thinking styles or motivation to think critically.

Association with Performance

Studies have focused largely on understanding factors that contribute to CT, as opposed to the consequences of CT. For example, in the following discussion of the malleability of CT, we note that there are numerous studies of the effects of training on acquisition of CT skills. However, we have not found studies examining the association of CT skills or dispositions with leader or job performance.[6]

---

[6] Rueb, Erskine, and Foti (2008) examined the association of CT skills and leadership among officers attending Air Force Squadron Officer School, but in this study, leadership was operationalized in terms of academic performance. Therefore, these findings pertain more to the association of CT skills and intellectual constructs such as GMA.

However, some research has shown that CT skills are related to cognitive processes that influence judgment and decisionmaking, providing indirect evidence of a possible association of CT and leader or job performance. West and his colleagues found that people with high scores on a test of CT skills showed fewer common cognitive biases (West, Toplak, and Stanovich, 2008). Cognitive biases are "rules of thumb" that people use to make judgments under conditions of uncertainty. These rules of thumb are cognitively efficient, but they lead to predictable errors in judgment, which in turn influence decisions in a wide range of domains. Butler et al. (2012) found that college students and adults who scored higher on a test of CT skills reported fewer negative life events in a range of domains, suggesting that higher CT skills are associated with better decisionmaking in real-world situations.[7] It is reasonable to expect a similar association for Army leaders, but the link between CT and military judgment and decisionmaking is an open research question.

Malleability

There is substantial evidence that training can influence CT skills. In military environments, Cohen and his colleagues have developed CT skills training and have shown improvement in students' performance on decisionmaking tasks (Cohen et al., 2000). Fischer et al. (2008) found that a computerized CT skills training program produced improvement in one aspect of CT, evaluating the need for new information when assessing a situation. Griffin and McClary (2015) studied CT skills training in Army Human Terrain System education and found that students showed improvement in CT skills as measured by the Halpern Critical Thinking Assessment (Halpern, 2010). More generally, two meta-analyses by Abrami and colleagues (Abrami et al., 2008; 2015) show that CT instruction has a positive effect on CT skills, but the nature of the training matters. In an analysis of 161 effect sizes, Abrami et al. (2008) found that when instruction about CT is explicit,

[7] Life events were measured with an adaptation of the Decision Outcomes Inventory ([DOI]; Bruine de Bruin, Parker, and Fischhoff, 2007). The DOI measures 34 life outcomes. Examples include, "Threw out food or groceries you had bought because they went bad," "Quit a job after a week," "Had your driver's license taken away from you by the police," "Locked yourself out of your home," and "Loaned more than $50 to someone and never got it back."

there are large effects of instruction. In contrast, immersing students in content that requires CT without providing explicit instruction on CT has a small effect. Abrami et al. (2015) compared three instructional approaches: dialogue (the Socratic method and other forms of discussion); authentic instruction (e.g., applied problem-solving and simulations), and mentoring (e.g., one-on-one instruction such as tutoring or internships). In their meta-analysis of 341 effect sizes, Abrami and his colleagues found effects of instruction on CT skills were larger for content-specific rather than generic CT. They also found that authentic instruction, dialogue, and their combination produced significant improvement in CT skills compared to control conditions.[8] However, the combination of authentic instruction and dialogue with mentoring had a much larger effect. Abrami and his colleagues suggest that mentoring works as a catalyst, augmenting other strategies that are less successful if used alone.

There has been far less research on the malleability of dispositional aspects of CT. Abrami et al. (2015) also examined this topic in their meta-analysis and found only 25 relevant effect sizes. Furthermore, these effects were heterogeneous, suggesting that moderating factors, such as participant age or instructional methods, influence results, but there were not enough studies available to examine moderating effects. Overall, results show that CT interventions positively influence CT dispositions, but much more research is needed to address this question.

Measurement Tools

There are a number of established tests that measure general CT skills (as opposed to domain-specific CT skills). Table 2.1 reviews some of the commonly used tests and the CT skills that they measure. The Ennis-Weir test is free to use, and the other tests are commercial in nature. Some of these test publishers also provide measures of dispositional aspects of CT.

The tests shown in Table 2.1 vary in format. Most of the tests use forced-choice questions. However, some researchers argue constructed-

[8] Mentoring alone did not produce improvement in CT skills compared to control conditions.

Table 2.1
Examples of Critical-Thinking Skills Tests

Measure	Description
Watson-Glaser Critical Thinking Appraisal (Watson and Glaser, 1980)	Forced-choice test measuring recognizing assumptions, evaluating arguments, and drawing conclusions
California Critical Thinking Skills Test (Facione, 1990)	Forced-choice test measuring analysis, evaluation, inference, deduction, induction, and overall reasoning
Cornell Critical Thinking Test (Level Z) (Ennis and Millman, 2005)	Forced-choice test measuring induction, deduction, credibility, identification of assumptions, semantics, definition, and prediction in planning experiments
Ennis-Weir Critical Thinking Essay Test (Ennis and Weir, 1985)	Constructed-response test measuring argument appraisal and formulation (e.g., identifying reasons and assumptions, stating one's point, offering good reasons, avoiding weak arguments such as equivocation, irrelevance, and overgeneralization)
Halpern Critical Thinking Assessment (Halpern, 2010)	Test consisting of constructed- and forced-choice questions measuring verbal reasoning, argument analysis, thinking as hypothesis testing, likelihood and uncertainty, and decisionmaking and problem-solving

response questions, or a combination of forced-choice and constructed-response questions, produce better assessments of higher-order cognitive processes and better reflect the tasks in actual job settings (e.g., Ennis, 1993; Halpern, 2010; Ku, 2009). The Ennis-Weir Critical Thinking Essay Test uses constructed-response questions, and the Halpern Critical Thinking Assessment (Halpern, 2010) uses a combination of forced-choice and constructed-response questions. Given the lack of research addressing the association of CT with outcomes such as job performance, there is insufficient evidence to determine whether the additional costs of administering and scoring constructed-response tests are justified by producing better assessments of CT skills.

There are many items in the public domain measuring cognitive biases and heuristics, an aspect of CT skills (see example items in Table 2.2), and some researchers have created batteries of such items that have been used extensively in research (e.g., West, Toplak, and Stanovich, 2008).

Table 2.2
Examples of Items Assessing Cognitive Biases and Heuristics

Cognitive Bias or Heuristic	Source	Example	Correct answer
Base rate fallacy	Tversky and Kahneman (1974)	"Steve is very shy and withdrawn, invariably helpful but with very little interest in people or in the world of reality. A meek and tidy soul, he has a need for order and structure, and a passion for detail. Is Steve more likely to be a librarian or a farmer?"	Many respondents choose "librarian" because the description of Steve sounds similar to common images of a librarian. This response shows failure to consider the base rate, i.e., there are many more farmers than librarians in the United States. The ratio of male farmers to male librarians is even higher.
Conjunction fallacy	Tversky and Kahneman (1983)	"Linda is 31 years old, single, outspoken, and very bright. She majored in philosophy. As a student, she was deeply concerned with issues of discrimination and social justice, and also participated in anti-nuclear demonstrations. Which is more probable? (a) Linda is a bank teller. (b) Linda is a bank teller and is active in the feminist movement."	Some people will choose (b) because it sounds like a more representative description of Linda (a heuristic called "representativeness"; Kahneman and Tversky, 1972). The correct response is (a) because the probability of two events occurring together is lower than the probability of either event occurring alone.
Availability heuristic	Tversky and Kahneman (1973)	"If you sample a word at random from an English text, it is more likely that: (a) the word starts with the letter K, or (b) that K is its third letter?"	Many respondents choose (a) because words that start with K come more easily to mind (are more available), which in turn influences estimates of frequency. In fact, a typical passage of text has twice as many words in which K is the third letter.

Bruine de Bruin, Parker, and Fischhoff (2007) developed a test called Adult Decision-Making Competence (ADMC) that assesses other aspects of decisionmaking effectiveness. The ADMC is a forced-choice test that measures a number of aspects of decisionmaking proficiency: resistance to framing effects (consistency in judgments whether outcomes are framed as a gain or a loss); recognizing social norms; under or overconfidence (how well calibrated people are in understanding their own knowledge); applying decision rules; consistency in risk perception (understanding rules of probability); and resistance to sunk costs. Bruine de Bruin, Parker, and Fischhoff (2007) showed that responses to the ADMC are associated with related constructs such as GMA and decisionmaking styles. The ADMC has also been used in other studies of decisionmaking (e.g., Del Missier, Mantyla, and Bruine de Bruin, 2010; Parker, Bruine de Bruin, and Fischhoff, 2007).

There are many affective or dispositional measures of cognitive or thinking styles or motivations to think critically. These measures are self-report instruments assessing one's propensity to engage in critical thinking, but they are not measures of CT skills. Two examples, the Actively Open-Minded Thinking Scale (AOT) (Stanovich and West, 1998) and the Need for Cognition Scale (Cacioppo, Petty, Feinstein, and Jarvis, 1996), are shown in Table 2.3. These and other thinking disposition scales—such as need for closure, dogmatism, reflectivity, superstitious thinking, and consideration of future consequences—have been associated with CT or other cognitive abilities in many empirical studies (see Toplak, West, and Stanovich, 2014).

Metacognition

Definition

Metacognition can be defined as "thinking about thinking" and refers to self-awareness about one's cognitive and problem-solving processes (Davidson, Deuser, and Sternberg, 1994; Flavell, 1979).[9]

---

[9] In this review, we focus on metacognition as awareness of one's cognitive processes. We note that a large body of work in education focuses on metacognition as awareness and

Table 2.3
Examples of Dispositional Measures of Critical Thinking

Measure	Description	Example Items
AOT Scale (Stanovich and West, 1998)	Forty-one items assessing cognitive flexibility and openness to changing one's beliefs, rated on six-point scales ranging from 1 = strongly disagree to 6 = strongly agree	• "People should always take into consideration evidence that goes against their beliefs." • "No one can talk me out of something I know is right." (reverse scored)
Need for Cognition Scale (Cacioppo, Petty, Feinstein, and Jarvis, 1996)	Eighteen items assessing the extent to which respondents enjoy and engage in cognitive endeavors. Respondents rate the extent to which items are characteristic of them on five-point scales ranging from "extremely uncharacteristic" to "extremely characteristic."	• "I would prefer complex to simple problems." • "Thinking is not my idea of fun." (reverse scored)

Association with Performance

In their review of metacognition and leadership, Marshall-Mies et al. (2000) argue that metacognitive skills are critical for effective leadership, given that leadership involves solving complex problems and metacognitive processes guide effective problem-solving. Metacognitive skills influence problem-solving by fostering: (1) understanding of the problem and its key parameters; (2) the search for and evaluation of solutions; and (3) monitoring implementation of solutions and adapting solutions in response to feedback (Marshall-Mies et al., 2000). Metacognition is associated with expertise in that experts engage in more metacognitive activities than novices do (see Phillips, Klein, and Sieck, 2004). The importance of metacognitive skills for senior leaders has been documented in Army research (Lucas and Markessini, 1993).

conscious use of *learning strategies* (e.g., Jacobson, 1998). Many researchers studying metacognition in educational settings assert that instructional practices can foster metacognitive skills (e.g., Jacobson, 1998; Schraw, 1998). Measures such as the Motivated Strategies for Learning Questionnaire (Pintrich, Smith, Garcia, and McKeachie, 1993) assess metacognition with respect to learning.

Metacognitive skills are posited to foster situational awareness (Cohen, Freeman, and Wolf, 1996; Endsley, 2000); in turn, there is evidence for the importance of situational awareness in leader adaptive performance. In his book on psychology in war, Matthews (2014) links situational awareness to tactical decisionmaking skills, arguing that higher awareness increases the likelihood of success. In a study of near-miss incidents among firefighters, continually assessing the environment, challenging assumptions, and checking work were all activities that contributed to a leader's success in dangerous situations (Baran and Scott, 2010). Aude et al. (2014) cite a number of other studies reporting a positive relationship between situational awareness and adaptive performance (Pleban et al., 2009; Strater, Jones, and Endsley, 2001; Saus et al., 2006). More recent evidence has shown that metacognitive skill influences the effects of job experiences on aspects of adaptive performance, including social competence and tacit leader knowledge. Zaccaro et al. (2009) reported that the positive effects of having challenging and diverse work experience on social competence were stronger for military leaders with higher metacognitive skills. Similarly, the association between challenging work assignments and tacit leader knowledge was positive and stronger for leaders with higher metacognitive skills.[10]

Malleability

A paucity of research exists on the malleability of metacognitive skills in the workplace. Much of the metacognitive training literature instead focuses on clinical or academic settings (e.g., McCabe, 2011; Moritz et al., 2011).[11] Therefore, the conclusions that we can draw are quite tentative. Nevertheless, there is some evidence that metacognitive skills are malleable. Research on expertise as mentioned and to be described in more detail later in this chapter provides indirect evidence for the malleability of metacognition in that experts engage in more metacognitive

---

[10] We did not find studies of the association of metacognition and job performance more generally.

[11] Geiwitz (1995) designed metacognitive training for officers; however, an evaluation of this training was not reported.

activities than do novices, and expertise develops through training, education, and experience. This suggests that metacognitive skills accrue with domain knowledge and skills—but becoming an expert takes a long time (Ericsson, 2006).

Schmidt and Ford (2003) studied a metacognitive intervention directly. Their results suggest that the benefits of the intervention for metacognitive activity and learning outcomes depend on individual differences such as learning goal orientation. In this study, students participated in training to create web pages; in the experimental condition, a 10-minute intervention on metacognitive activity preceded the primary training, and in the control group, there was no metacognitive intervention. Results showed that individuals who were less concerned about demonstrating incompetence (low avoidance orientation) showed greater metacognitive activity and greater declarative knowledge about the primary task after metacognitive training. In comparison, those who were concerned with demonstrating incompetence (high avoidance orientation) showed lower metacognitive activity and lower levels of declarative knowledge after metacognitive training. In addition, Schmidt and Ford (2003) found that greater metacognitive activity was associated with greater acquisition of declarative knowledge, higher self-efficacy, and superior performance on a skill-based measure. Schmidt and Ford (2003) propose ways in which these results can be used to enhance training outcomes. One approach is to customize the training to fit the learner's characteristics, e.g., by providing more metacognitive prompts to low-avoidance trainees and fewer prompts to high-avoidance trainees. A second approach is to change the learner to fit the training, e.g., by modifying the learner's performance-avoidance cognitions and behaviors. This approach, however, depends on a better understanding of the extent to which learning goal orientation is more state-like (rather than trait-like) and, therefore, more amenable to change.

Measurement Tools

Measuring metacognition is challenging because it is complex and unobservable, and it may be influenced by respondents' verbal abilities and aspects of GMA (Lai, 2011).

In some research, metacognitive skills have been evaluated through interviews, think-aloud strategies during problem-solving, or testing (see Marshall-Mies et al., 2000; Schraw and Dennison, 1994). These approaches typically infer use of metacognitive strategies in participants' responses as evaluated by subject matter experts (SMEs). Thus, these methods are not scalable when assessing large numbers of personnel.

There are a number of self-report instruments assessing metacognition, but most are designed for academic learning contexts and are geared toward children. In contrast, Schraw and Dennison (1994) developed and tested the Metacognitive Awareness Inventory (MAI), which is designed for older students and adults, and many of the items on this scale may be appropriate for basic and applied Army research. The MAI consists of 52 items measuring two related categories of metacognition: knowledge of cognition (awareness of one's cognitive strengths and weaknesses) and regulation of cognition (planning, implementing, monitoring, and evaluating use of strategies). While many of the MAI items are related to classroom learning (e.g., "I am aware of what strategies I use while I study" and "I know what the teacher expects me to learn"), a number of items address cognitive processes more generally or pertain to problem-solving (e.g., "I understand my intellectual strengths and weaknesses" and "I ask myself if I have considered all options when solving a problem"). Studies of the MAI with college students show that scores on the MAI were correlated with actual knowledge and test performance.

Creative Problem-Solving

Definition

In defining innovation, ADRP 6-22 emphasizes the need for leaders to produce creative ideas and solve problems effectively. In this review, we focus our discussion of creativity largely on innovative or creative problem-solving and divergent thinking. Creative problem-solving entails generating solutions to novel, complex, and ill-defined problems (Eubanks, Murphy, and Mumford, 2010; Scott, Lonergan, and Mumford, 2005; Vincent, Decker, and Mumford, 2002). Work in this area has identified five key processing activities that contribute to creative problem-solving: problem-construction or problem-finding, information gathering, conceptual combination, idea generation, and idea evaluation (e.g., Scott, Lonergan, and Mumford, 2005). Theories of personality also point to dispositional characteristics related to creative problem-solving. A dominant theory of personality is the Five-Factor Model or "Big Five," a taxonomy consisting of five broad personality factors: extraversion, emotional stability, agreeableness, conscientiousness, and openness to experience (e.g., Digman, 1990). Openness to experience, which includes facets such as curiosity, ingenuity, and intellectual efficiency (e.g., Drasgow et al., 2012), has been linked to creativity and innovation in prior research.

Association with Performance

Zaccaro et al. (2000) studied complex problem-solving skills among 1,807 Army officers in grades O1 to O6 who were enrolled in Army officer education courses. While providing evidence for the validity of a number of measures, the data also shed light on the relationships among problem-solving skills, creativity, and leadership. Complex problem-solving skills (both cued, question prompts provided, and uncued, scenario only without prompts) were significantly correlated with divergent thinking and officer career achievement.[12] Tremble, Kane, and Stewart (1997) found similar results among officers in the chains of command of 53 battalions in that the process of problem construction was predictive of career achievement, but problem-solving skills were not associated with leader performance as assessed by superiors and subordinates.

Two other studies use a subset of the Zaccaro et al. (2000) data to examine divergent thinking and creativity among Army leaders. Vincent, Decker, and Mumford (2002) found that divergent thinking ("the

[12] Complex problem-solving skills were measured through three scenarios that required a constructed (open-ended) response. They were each rated on their use of eight problem-solving processing skills from the Mumford et al. (1991) taxonomy of creative problem-solving: problem construction, information encoding, category search, category specification, category combination and reorganization, idea evaluation, solution implementation, and solution monitoring.

ability to generate multiple alternative problem solutions," p. 163) was highly correlated with idea generation and with idea implementation and moderately correlated with leader performance.[13] Vincent, Decker, and Mumford (2002) also found that intelligence and expertise were positively associated with divergent thinking. Connelly et al. (2000) showed that creative thinking and creative writing (but not verbal reasoning) significantly predicted leader achievement (i.e., rank) in the Army.

Studies of dispositions show that openness to experience is associated with leader and job performance. A meta-analysis of the Big Five factors (Judge et al., 2002) found that openness to experience predicted both leader emergence and leader effectiveness. More recently, a meta-analysis showed that openness to experience is associated with job performance, particularly for jobs that are unstructured, where personnel have decisionmaking discretion, or there is a strong requirement for innovation or creativity (Judge and Zapata, 2015).

Malleability

Research suggests that creative problem-solving skills are not fixed. The importance of domain-relevant or technical expertise is widely acknowledged in theories and empirical research on leadership and creativity (see Mumford, Connelly, and Gaddis, 2003, for a review). As we discuss later in this chapter, and as described in ADRP 6-22, expertise develops through job experience, training, and education, suggesting that creativity is malleable, at least in part. Moreover, there is evidence that creativity can be trained. A meta-analysis of 70 studies by Scott, Leritz, and Mumford (2004) found that creativity training had positive effects across age groups, organizational settings, and intellectual capabilities. Specifically, gains were found in divergent thinking, problem-solving, performance, and attitudes and behaviors. Scott, Leritz and Mumford (2004) also examined the relationship between course content, delivery methods, and positive outcomes. Results yielded four evidence-based recommendations for designing and implementing creativity

---

[13] Leader performance was measured by an index including number of medals and citations, prior performance evaluations, promotions ahead of schedule, and admission to special training programs.

training: (1) use training based on a valid cognitive framework (e.g., Mumford et al., 1991); (2) provide lengthy and challenging training with attention to the association between underlying cognitive skills and how they influence creativity; (3) illustrate material about cognitive skills with real-world contextual examples; and (4) follow instruction about cognitive skills and examples with practical exercises that give participants opportunities to apply strategies within a relevant domain.

In contrast to skills, dispositional aspects of creativity are more fixed. Many theories in psychology have argued that personality development takes place in childhood and adolescence but remains relatively unchanged in adulthood. In light of research linking Big Five characteristics to creativity, this might suggest that creativity is relatively stable over time. However, more recent longitudinal studies conclude that some Big Five factors continue to change throughout adulthood (Roberts, Walton, and Viechtbauer, 2006; Helson et al., 2002), although the exact nature of the changes has been described as a complex phenomenon and highly variable across individuals (Srivastava et al., 2003).

A meta-analysis of 92 studies of longitudinal changes in the Big Five traits concluded that different traits are likely to change at different points during the lifespan (Roberts et al., 2006). Of particular interest for this report is change during ages 18 to 22 (which Roberts and his colleagues refer to as the college years) and ages 22 to 30 (the first decade of young adulthood), the periods over which most formative training in the military occurs. Results of Roberts, Walton, and Viechtbauer (2006) show significant increases in openness to experience during young adulthood but no changes in subsequent decades (and decreases in individuals ages 60 to 70). However, the cause of these changes is not well understood.

Measurement Tools

There are a number of different approaches to measuring creative problem-solving and related constructs. The most common approach to measuring creativity includes assessments in which respondents' answers are rated on a predetermined set of criteria. All these tests use constructed-response questions.

Table 2.4
Examples of General Creativity Tests and Measures of Behaviors and Achievements

Measure	Description
Consequences Test (Christensen, Merrifield, and Guilford, 1953)	Constructed-response test in which respondents identify potential consequences of hypothetical events, such as gravity being cut in half. Responses are scored by three judges who rate the quality and originality on a five-point scale.
Alternate Uses Test (Wallach and Kogan, 1965)	Constructed-response test in which respondents generate as many unusual uses as they can for common objects, such as a brick, or identify as many common items as they can that share a feature, such as having a wheel. Responses are rated for originality, fluency, flexibility, and elaboration.
Biographical Inventory of Creative Behaviors (Batey, 2007)	Self-assessment in which respondents answer yes or no to indicate involvement across 34 activities ranging from creative writing to leadership or coaching.
Creative Behavior Inventory (Hocevar, 1979; Dollinger, 2003)	Self-assessment in which respondents indicate how often they have engaged in each of 28 artistic activities, such as "Designed and made your own greeting cards" and "Wrote the lyrics to a song," with four-point response options ranging from "never did this" to "did this more than five times."
Creative Domain Questionnaire-Revised (Kaufman, Cole, and Baer, 2009)	Self-assessment in which respondents report self-perceptions of their creativity in 56 domains spanning a wide range of topics, e.g., dance, music, art, business, science, and interpersonal relations, rated on six-point scales ranging from "not at all creative" to "extremely creative."

In the Zaccaro et al. (2000) study of creative problem-solving, respondents were presented with military scenarios to read. One of the scenarios (cued) was accompanied by response questions, while the other (uncued) was not. Trained raters assessed the cued responses on the following problem-solving processes: problem construction, information encoding, category search, category combination and reorganization, idea evaluation, solution implementation, and solution monitoring. The uncued responses were rated for overall quality and originality by trained judges.

Table 2.4 lists other commonly used, domain-general measures of creativity. Some of these instruments are tests in which respondents are asked to generate ideas, which are then judged for quality. Other measures consist of self-report assessments, in which respondents answer questions about their behaviors, accomplishments, or self-beliefs across various domains of creativity. While acceptable for low-stakes settings, Silvia et al. (2012) caution that self-report assessments may not be appropriate for high-stakes use, such as personnel selection, due to their susceptibility to "faking good," i.e., whereby respondents answer questions to present the impression of being more creative than they actually are.

Table 2.5 provides examples of self-report instruments of dispositional aspects of creativity. As mentioned in the discussion of CT skills, dispositional measures are not a replacement for measuring skills but reflect the propensity to engage in relevant behaviors.

The Creative Personality Scale (CPS) (Gough, 1979) is specific to creativity. The other measures in Table 2.5 are instruments that assess openness to experience and the other Big Five traits, several of which are relevant to other attributes discussed later in this report. The International Personality Item Pool (IPIP) consists of a variety of personality inventories (Goldberg, 1999). The IPIP website ("International Personality Item Pool," 2017) has over 2,400 items that can be used to measure facets of the Big Five or the Big Five factors overall.

The remaining instruments are commercially available. The NEO[14] Personality Inventory - Revised (NEO PI-R) (Costa and McCrae, 1992) and the Hogan Personality Inventory (HPI) (Hogan and Hogan, 1995) have been widely used in research and practice.[15] The Tailored Adaptive Personality Assessment System (TAPAS) was developed for the Army (Stark et al., 2014). In contrast to many other instruments that use single statements with Likert-type response options, the TAPAS was designed to be more resistant to faking good by using paired comparisons. That is, the respondent is presented with pairs of statements reflecting different facets and is asked to select the statement that is "more

[14] Originally "Neuroticism-Extraversion-Openness," now called "NEO."

[15] The HPI uses somewhat different labels for the Big Five: adjustment (emotional stability); sociability and ambition (extraversion); likeability (agreeableness); prudence (conscientiousness); and intellectance (openness to experience) (see Salgado, Moscoso, and Alonso, 2013). The HPI includes an additional factor, School Success, which measures enjoyment of academic activities and value of educational achievement.

Table 2.5
Examples of Dispositional Measures of Creativity or Related Constructs

Measure	Description	Example Items
CPS (Gough, 1979)	Respondents indicate which adjectives describe themselves among 300 potential descriptors from the Adjective Check List (Gough and Heilbrun, 1965). The CPS measures creativity potential based on responses to 30 of the items.	• "Inventive" • "Unconventional" • "Cautious" (reverse scored) • "Conventional" (reverse scored)
IPIP (Goldberg et al., 1999)	Measures multiple facets of each of the Big Five. Respondents are presented with brief behavioral descriptions and rate how accurately each statement describes them using a five-point Likert-type scale ranging from "very inaccurate" to "very accurate."	• "Have a vivid imagination" (openness to experience) • "Am quiet around strangers" (extraversion) • "Am interested in people" (agreeableness) • "Pay attention to details" (conscientiousness)
NEO PI-R (Costa and McCrae, 1992)	This is a commercial instrument consisting of 240 descriptive items measuring six facets of each of the Big Five. Respondents rate their agreement with descriptive statements using a five-point Likert scale ranging from "strongly disagree" to "strongly agree." Facets of openness to experience include fantasy, aesthetics, feelings, actions, ideas, and values. There are several other versions of the NEO, including a short version, the NEO Five-Factor Inventory (McCrae and Costa, 2004).	• "I often try new, foreign foods" • "I find philosophical arguments boring" (reverse scored) • "I have a lot of intellectual curiosity"
HPI (Hogan and Hogan, 1995)	This is a commercial instrument consisting of 206 true-false questions measuring multiple facets of six dimensions based on the Five-Factor Model. Respondents rate their agreement with descriptive statements using true-false options. Facets of intellectance or inquisitiveness include imagination, curiosity, and creative potential.	• "I am a quick-witted person" • "I have taken things apart just to see how they work"
TAPAS (Stark et al., 2014)	This is a commercial instrument developed for the Army. Uses paired comparisons to measure up to 22 facets of the Big Five. Facets of openness to experience include intellectual efficiency, curiosity, ingenuity, aesthetic, tolerance, and depth.	• Two items in a pair include, "I am known as a 'quick thinker'" (from one of the facets in the openness to experience domain) and "I get along well with coworkers" (from one of the facets in the agreeableness domain) (Stark et al., 2014).

like me." The two statements in each pair are chosen to be similar in social desirability (see Table 2.5). Online administration of the TAPAS uses computer-adaptive testing (CAT), or tailored testing, in which a respondent's answers influence the subsequent items that are presented. Using CAT provides accurate measurement with fewer items compared to paper-and-pencil tests. However, the TAPAS can also be administered in a traditional paper-and-pencil format. The TAPAS has been used for applicant screening among Army recruits at Military Entrance Processing Stations (MEPS) beginning in 2009 as well for research with Air Force and Navy recruits (Stark et al., 2014). Drasgow et al. (2012) showed similar scores for military personnel in a high stakes environment (Army applicants who took the TAPAS for enlistment screening) and a low stakes environment (Air Force applicants who took the TAPAS for research purposes only). This finding suggests that the TAPAS is resistant to faking good.

Self-report instruments are often used in organizations to measure personality traits, but personality traits can also be measured through others' assessments of targets. A series of three meta-analyses by Connelly and Ones (2010) showed that other-ratings can improve the accuracy of personality ratings and can enhance predictive validities of job performance. The nature of the personality trait being assessed, interpersonal intimacy between the raters and the target, and the number of other-raters are important factors in using other-ratings.

Emotional Intelligence

Definition

The concept of emotional intelligence (EI) has been the focus of substantial attention in the psychology and management literatures over the past twenty years. EI appears to map on to the intellectual attribute of "interpersonal tact" in the ALRM as well as attributes in presence and character categories; i.e., confidence and empathy, respectively. However, as noted by Spector and Johnson (2006, p. 325), "There is perhaps no construct in the social sciences that has produced more controversy in recent years than emotional intelligence." The conceptual definition (and measurement) of EI continues to be hotly debated (e.g., see Society for Industrial and Organizational Psychology [2010] for a scholarly dialogue). With this in mind, we outline the two primary models of EI as described by Joseph and Newman (2010): *ability* and *mixed* emotional intelligence.[16]

Ability EI corresponds to a type of cognitive ability reflecting the aptitude to perform tasks and solve problems involving one's own emotions and those of others (Côté, 2014; Mayer and Salovey, 1993). For example, a definition of EI from this "conceptual camp" is "the ability to carry out accurate reasoning about emotions and the ability to use emotions and emotional knowledge to enhance thought" (Mayer, Roberts, and Barsade, 2008, p. 507). The most commonly cited model in this paradigm is Mayer and Salovey's (1997) four branch, hierarchical model: (1) perceiving and expressing emotions, (2) using emotion, (3) understanding emotions, and (4) regulating emotions. Constructs such as empathy, creative thinking, and flexible planning are subsumed in this view of EI (Salovey and Mayer, 1990).

Mixed EI is an "umbrella term that encompasses a constellation of personality traits, affect, and self-perceived abilities" (Joseph, Jin, Newman, and O'Boyle, 2015, p. 298) drawing from the models of Bar-On (1997), Goleman (1995), and Petrides and Furnham (2001). These traits and abilities include, but are not limited to, assertiveness, optimism, and stress tolerance.

Association with Performance

Multiple meta-analyses have analyzed the association of EI and leader or job performance. A meta-analysis of 48 studies (99 correlations) found a moderately strong correlation between EI and leadership effectiveness (Mills, 2009). However, this study did not differentiate between ability and mixed EI measures. Another meta-analysis of 62 correlations examined the association between EI and transformational leadership

[16] Mixed emotional intelligence has also been referred to as trait emotional intelligence.

(Harms and Credé, 2010).[17] Ability measures of EI showed smaller relationships with transformational leadership than did trait measures; however, these moderate to strong correlations occurred only when leaders self-assessed their EI and transformational leadership. When these ratings came from different sources (e.g., leader self-assessments of EI and subordinate ratings of transformational leadership), the associations approached zero. Thus, the stronger associations could be a result of common-method bias and/or social desirability in leaders' responses to both measures rather than because of a true association between EI and transformational leadership.[18]

Several meta-analyses have examined emotional intelligence and job performance more generally. Estimates of the relationship are moderately small, and results depend on factors such as how EI and job performance are conceptualized and measured (Joseph and Newman, 2010; O'Boyle et al., 2011; Van Rooy and Viswesvaran, 2004). For example, findings from Joseph and Newman (2010) indicate that the association of ability EI and performance depends on the type of job, such that EI predicts performance in occupations with high emotional labor (jobs requiring frequent interpersonal interaction) but not in occupations with low emotional labor. In contrast, Joseph and Newman (2010) found positive associations of mixed EI and performance across jobs, but EI overlapped substantially with other well-established constructs (such as the Big Five). Most recently, a meta-analysis by Joseph, Jin, Newman, and O'Boyle (2015) found that the relationship of mixed EI and job performance could be accounted for by a combination of traits known to predict performance, such as Big Five factors and cognitive ability.

---

[17] A transformational leader inspires and empowers followers to move beyond their self-interests and act in ways that benefit the group or organization (e.g., Bass, 1985). In contrast, a transactional leader focuses on gaining compliance from followers through the use of rewards and punishments.

[18] Common method bias occurs when the same type of method or measure (e.g., self-report) is used for predictor and outcome variables. As a result, the correlation between the variables may be influenced by the method of assessment as opposed to by the substance of the constructs being measured.

Malleability

Given the ongoing debate surrounding EI, many scholars remain skeptical about whether EI can be enhanced (e.g., Landy, 2005). Some recent studies report notable improvements in participants' EI after participating in training programs (e.g., Boyatzis and Saatcioglu, 2008; Grant, 2007; Groves, McEnrue, and Shen, 2006). However, results should be interpreted with caution in light of conceptual and methodological issues in EI theory and research. Many of the EI development interventions have been criticized for weak theoretical foundations and inadequate evaluation, e.g., relying only on trainees' subjective reports and/or failing to include control groups (Nelis et al., 2009). For example, Boyatzis and Saatcioglu (2008) conducted 14 longitudinal studies of the impact of an MBA program on developing EI. The authors concluded that these competencies can be developed in adults and improvements can be sustained as long as seven years. However, given that these studies did not have control or other comparison groups, one cannot attribute changes in EI to the MBA program. Nelis and colleagues (2009) conducted a controlled experiment involving undergraduate students who received EI training focusing on EI knowledge and skills. The training consisted of two and one-half hour sessions conducted weekly for four weeks. In comparison to a no-training control group, participants in the treatment group showed improvement in measures of EI immediately following training and six months later. However, the sample size of the study was small and results varied for different EI measures in the study. Thus, we conclude that evidence for the malleability of EI through training and education remains equivocal.

Measurement Tools

Different methods are used to assess EI. The most common methods include objective tests, self-report questionnaires, and 360-degree evaluations. Table 2.6 presents a brief summary of the instruments commonly used to assess EI according to various meta-analyses.

Table 2.6
Examples of Measures of Emotional Intelligence

Measure	Description
Ability EI	
Mayer–Salovey–Caruso Emotional Intelligence Test (MSCEIT) (Mayer et al., 2003)	MSCEIT V2.0 is a commercial test consisting of 141 items designed to measure four dimensions: (1) perceiving emotions, (2) using emotions to facilitate thought, (3) understanding emotions, and (4) managing emotions. For example, in the "faces" task, participants view a series of faces and indicate the degree to which a specific emotion is present. Each dimension is measured with two tasks; therefore, there are eight distinct tasks. Response options vary (e.g., five-point rating scales, multiple-choice response formats).
Wong and Law Emotional Intelligence Scale (Wong and Law, 2002)	WLEIS is a self-report questionnaire that contains 16 items measuring four facets: (1) self-emotion appraisal (e.g., "I have a good sense of why I have certain feelings most of the time."), (2) others' emotion appraisal (e.g., "I always know my friends' emotions from their behavior."), (3) use of emotion (e.g., "I always set goals for myself and then try my best to achieve them."), and (4) regulation of emotion (e.g., "I am able to control my temper and handle difficulties rationally."). Response options follow a seven-point Likert-type scale ranging from "strongly agree" to "strongly disagree."
Mixed EI	
Emotional Quotient Inventory (EQ-I), (Bar-On, 2006)	EQ-I is a commercial, self-report questionnaire consisting of 133 items designed to measure five composite scales: (1) intrapersonal (e.g., assertiveness, independence), (2) interpersonal (e.g., empathy, social responsibility), (3) stress management (stress tolerance and impulse control), (4) adaptability (e.g., flexibility, problem-solving), and (5) general mood (optimism and happiness). The items consist of short sentences. Five-point response scale range from (1) "very seldom or not true of me" to (5) "very often true of me or true of me." The EQ-I takes approximately 40 minutes to complete. This test is proprietary, and example items are not available.
Emotional Competence Inventory (ECI) (Boyatzis and Sala, 2004)	ECI-2 is a commercial, 360-degree questionnaire that contains 72 items assessing four clusters, each of which comprises multiple competencies. The clusters and examples of competencies include: (1) self-awareness (e.g., self-confidence, accurate self-assessment), (2) self-management (e.g., adaptability, optimism), (3) social awareness (e.g., empathy, organizational awareness), and (4) relationship management or social skills (e.g., developing others, conflict management). The measure can be administered to an individual's boss, peers, and subordinates at work as well as spouses, friends, and clients. This test is proprietary, and example items are not available.

Expertise

Definition

ADRP 6-22 defines expertise as "the special knowledge and skill developed from experience, training, and education," and identifies four types of domain knowledge: tactical, technical, joint, and cultural and geopolitical.[19] In research, expertise is typically defined in terms of job knowledge and skills. Individuals with higher levels of expertise have greater *declarative knowledge* (factual knowledge) and *procedural knowledge* (how to perform tasks) (Anderson, 1983; Dye, Reck, and McDaniel, 1993). *Tacit knowledge* is a type of procedural knowledge; it refers to knowledge that is implicit or not readily articulated. Tacit knowledge is reflected in stronger perceptual skills, more complex mental models, the ability to quickly recognize and interpret associations or patterns in sets of information, and having larger repertoires of strategies to complete tasks in a particular domain (see Phillips, Klein, and Sieck, 2004, for a review). Sternberg and his colleagues (e.g., Sternberg and Wagner, 1993; Wagner and Sternberg, 1985), refer to tacit knowledge as an indicator of practical intelligence, which is related to, but distinct from GMA.

Association with Performance

We have found little research examining the association of leader expertise (being an expert in leadership) and leader performance. One exception is Hedlund et al. (2003), who studied tacit knowledge among Army leaders at platoon, company, and battalion levels. Hedlund et al. (2003) developed an instrument, Tacit Knowledge for Military Leaders (TKML), and studied the association of performance on the test with GMA and job performance ratings (see also Antonakis et al., 2002). Results were mixed in that the association of TKML scores and job performance depended on the nature of the relationship between the target individuals and raters (i.e., subordinates, peers, or superiors).

[19] Tactical knowledge pertains to the use of military means to accomplish a designated objective; technical knowledge refers to specialized information about a function or system; joint knowledge reflects an understanding of joint organizations and their roles and procedures in national defense, and cultural and geopolitical knowledge is an awareness of cultural, geographic, and political differences and sensitivities (Headquarters, Department of the Army, 2012b, p. 5-3).

For example, for platoon leaders, TKML scores were positively associated with supervisor ratings but not with peer ratings; for company commanders, TKML scores were associated with peer ratings but not with supervisor or subordinate ratings. Also, experience (months in current position) was not correlated with TKML scores at any level, which Hedlund et al. (2003) attribute to methodological limitations of the study rather than to a lack of a true association of experience and tacit knowledge.

Some studies have examined the association of domain-specific knowledge and experience with adaptive performance among leaders. In a study of firefighters and near-miss incidents, Baran and Scott (2010) showed that previous knowledge and experience influenced the ability of leaders to adapt and succeed in dangerous contexts. More broadly, Pulakos et al. (2002) found that past experience in situations requiring individuals to be adaptive was associated with subsequent ratings of adaptive performance. Mueller-Hanson et al. (2005) hypothesize that repeated experience in the same situation may not foster performance in novel situations (and, in fact, may hurt performance, e.g., Dane, 2010; Sternberg and Frensch, 1992); instead, they argue that experience in a variety of situations requiring change is beneficial to adaptive performance. We address ostensible trade-offs between expertise and adaptive performance in the final chapter of this report.

In terms of job performance more generally, there is a considerable body of work on the association of domain expertise and experience with performance in diverse contexts; a review of this literature exceeds the scope of this report (for a comprehensive resource, see Ericsson et al., 2006). However, several meta-analyses have examined expertise and job performance. Schmidt and Hunter (1998) showed that job knowledge is moderately to strongly associated with job performance across a range of jobs, whereas job experience has small to moderate associations with performance across jobs (see also Hunter and Hunter, 1984; McDaniel, Schmidt, and Hunter, 1988; Quiñones, Ford, and Teachout, 1995).[20] More specifically, studies of informal procedural

[20] There are a number of factors, including level of experience, job complexity, and opportunities to perform key tasks, that moderate the association of experience and performance.

knowledge show that scores on tests of tacit knowledge predict performance across a range of occupations, such as business managers, college professors, and salespeople (see Sternberg, 1999, for a review).

Malleability

Expertise develops through formal training, education, and job experience. Becoming an *expert* takes substantial time and deliberate practice (e.g., Horn and Masunaga, 2006; Ericsson, 2006). Ericsson's research (e.g., Ericsson, Krampe, and Tesch-Romer, 1993; Ericsson, 2006) indicates that becoming an expert takes approximately 10,000 hours or 10 years of deliberate practice. Deliberate practice is focused and programmatic; it entails repetition of the task over extended periods of time; setting specific, difficult goals; seeking immediate and objective feedback; and using the feedback to correct errors and set more challenging goals (e.g., Ericsson, 2006; Horn and Masanuga, 2006; see also Phillips, Klein, and Sieck, 2004).

Tacit knowledge typically develops outside of formal training. For example, leaders may learn about strategies for managing others through formal training, but they learn about the effectiveness of those strategies through experience and vicarious learning (e.g., Antonakis et al., 2002; Hedlund et al., 2003; Sternberg, 1999; Wagner and Sternberg, 1985). Being able to reflect on those experiences is also important (Phillips, Klein, and Sieck, 2004; Zaccaro et al., 2009). As noted earlier, Zaccaro et al. (2009) found that the association between challenging work assignments and tacit military leader knowledge was stronger for leaders with higher metacognitive skills (as well as higher levels of cognitive complexity). In addition, leaders play an important role in acquisition

The association of job experience and performance is stronger at lower levels (two to three years of experience) than at higher levels and has a nonlinear association, similar to other learning curves (e.g., McDaniel, Schmidt, and Hunter, 1988; Schmidt and Hunter, 1992). Sturman (2003) found that job experience was increasingly predictive of performance for jobs high in complexity, whereas the association of experience and performance was relatively constant for jobs low in complexity. Quiñones, Ford, and Teachout (1995) found that having more opportunities to perform relevant tasks was more strongly associated with performance than was job tenure or experience in similar types of jobs.

of others' tacit knowledge by serving as role models and coaching subordinates on the job (see Antonakis et al., 2002, for a review).

Clearly, motivation to learn and improve one's performance is an important factor in becoming an expert (Ericsson, 2006; Phillips, Klein, and Sieck, 2004). Aside from motivation, however, the other factors associated with developing expertise pose challenges in the realm of leadership. Many of Ericsson and colleagues' studies of expertise have been conducted with master chess players, athletes, and musicians. These are professions or activities in high-validity or predictable environments (Kahneman and Klein, 2009) that are conducive to repetition and allow for feedback that is relatively objective (Shanteau, 1992). In contrast, many leadership tasks are abstract and occur in environments that are unstructured, change rapidly, and lack objective feedback about outcomes. To facilitate learning about decisionmaking in ambiguous situations, Phillips, Klein, and Sieck (2004) propose using scenario-based training to give opportunities for practice, coupled with several feedback strategies: providing cognitive feedback (e.g., feedback about the associations of variables in the environment) and process feedback (information about the learner's approach to making decisions); having learners conduct observations and interviews to learn how SMEs make decisions; and combining practice with coaching.

Measurement Tools

Job knowledge typically is measured with written tests that are customized to a particular job or occupation. Tests can be multiple-choice or open-ended, as described in Chapter One of this report. For some jobs, commercial or open-source tests of job knowledge may already exist or new measures must be developed based on a job analysis.

Tacit knowledge has been assessed primarily with situational judgment tests (SJTs) (e.g., Antonakis et al., 2002; Hedlund et al., 2003; Wagner, 1987; Wagner and Sternberg, 1985). SJTs present realistic, hypothetical situations followed by multiple-choice questions in which the test-taker is asked how he or she might respond to the situation. SJTs are particularly appropriate for assessment of performance in situations that have more than one correct response. In contrast to multiple-choice tests of declarative or procedural knowledge that have clear-cut correct or incorrect responses, SJTs are much more labor-intensive to develop. The TKML (Antonakis et al., 2002; Hedlund et al., 2003), referenced earlier, is an SJT specific to assessing tacit knowledge among military leaders.

Work samples or hands-on performance tests are approaches to measuring some types of job *skills* as well as knowledge. Work samples are simulations of specific activities that approximate performance of an actual work situation (Lievens and De Soete, 2012). For example, asking test takers to write and deliver a briefing can provide measures of content knowledge and written and oral communication skills. Work samples can be especially useful for assessing attributes that are not easily captured in written tests. Work samples also have high face validity (test-takers view the tests as relevant to the job), so test takers tend to view these tests as job-related and fair (Callinan and Robertson, 2000). However, work samples have some disadvantages; they can be labor intensive to design, may need to be administered on an individual basis, may require use of specialized equipment, and may require SMEs to rate test performance. In addition, for some skills or tasks (e.g., using complex equipment or systems), individuals must have some degree of knowledge or experience before work samples can be used.

Interviews are also used to assess job knowledge. A meta-analysis has shown that interviews assessing specific job knowledge and skills have moderate validity in predicting job performance (Huffcutt et al., 2001). However, like many work samples, interviews are costly to conduct. In addition, interviews that lack structure and standardization—as often conducted in organizations—dramatically reduce validity (Huffcutt and Arthur, 1994). The validity of interviews for assessing job knowledge or other competencies can be improved by conducting structured interviews, in which questions are based on job analysis, and interviewers are trained, ask the same questions in each interview, and evaluate responses using rating scales with clearly defined anchors.

Intellect: Summary of Findings

Table 2.7 summarizes the findings regarding malleability and measurement of constructs associated with intellect.

Table 2.7
Summary of Research on Malleability and Common Measures: Intellect

Construct	Malleability	Common Measures
GMA	Evidence suggests that crystallized intelligence develops, in part, through training and education, but development is gradual. Development of fluid intelligence is largely normative in nature; it peaks in young adulthood (mid-20s) and declines gradually and monotonically through the remainder of life (with the possible exception of working memory, which does not decline or can be enhanced). Therefore, fluid intelligence is unlikely to change substantially through training.	Standardized tests such as the ASVAB, SAT, ACT, GRE; Wechsler Adult Intelligence Scale-IV (Wechsler, Coalson, and Raiford, 2008); Raven's Standard Progressive Matrices (Raven, Raven, and Court, 1998); Nelson-Denny Reading Test (Brown, Fishco, and Hanna, 1993); Miller Analogies Test (Pearson Assessment, 2016)
CT	There is strong evidence for positive effects of training on critical thinking skills, particularly when domain-specific; less (although positive) evidence for effects of training on dispositional aspects of critical thinking.	Standardized, multiple-choice commercial tests of domain-general critical thinking skills Self-report scales of dispositional aspects of CT, such as the AOT Scale (Stanovich and West, 1998) and the Need for Cognition Scale (Cacioppo, Petty, Feinstein, and Jarvis, 1996)
Metacognition	There is little research regarding the trainability of metacognitive skills outside of academic contexts.	The Metacognitive Awareness Inventory (Schraw and Dennison, 1994)
Creative problem-solving	There is strong evidence for positive effects of creativity training across diverse populations. Dispositional factors (openness to experience) increase in young adulthood, but the cause of these changes is not well understood.	Approaches to measuring creative problem-solving skills include creativity tests in which constructed response scenarios are rated by judges, self-report surveys of behaviors or biographic information. Self-report scales of the Big Five measure openness to experience (a dispositional factor associated with creative problem-solving).

Table 2.7—Continued

Construct	Malleability	Common Measures
EI	Numerous training programs have been implemented to develop EI, but there is a lack of robust research on the effectiveness of these interventions.	The WLEIS (Wong and Law, 2002) is a self-report measure. Other commonly used measures are commercial instruments and include the MSCEIT (Mayer et al., 2003), which is an objective test, and proprietary questionnaires: the EQ-I (Bar-On, 2006), which is self-report questionnaire, and the ECI (Boyatzis and Sala, 2004), which is a 360-degree questionnaire.
Expertise	Expertise develops through job experience, training, and education. Deliberate practice is a critical factor contributing to becoming an expert in a particular domain.	Knowledge is measured with customized written tests, work samples, SJTs, and interviews.

CHAPTER THREE

Presence Attributes

In the ALRM, *presence* refers to how others perceive leaders in terms of outward appearance and behavior (Headquarters, Department of the Army, 2012b). According the ALRM, a leader's presence can inspire followers to do their best. We review four constructs related to presence: physical fitness, generalized self-efficacy, extraversion, and resilience. The chapter is organized according to each construct. Again, we define each and discuss the construct according to findings related directly to leadership and general job performance or related outcomes. We then review findings related to the malleability of the construct, and, finally, we present specific measures. We summarize the findings in Table 3.3.

Physical Fitness

Definition

Although there is no universally agreed upon definition of physical fitness and its components, experts generally agree that physical fitness is "a set of attributes that relate to the ability of people to perform physical activity" (McArdle, Katch, and Katch, 1991, as cited in Knapik et al., 2006, p. 615). Perhaps the most parsimonious conceptualization of physical fitness is Hogan's (1991) definition, which consists of muscular strength, cardiovascular endurance, and movement quality. A more comprehensive taxonomy followed by the National Strength and Conditioning Association for military physical readiness categorizes components as health-related (muscular strength, muscular endurance, aerobic fitness, flexibility, body composition) or skill-related (agility, balance, coordination, power, reaction time, and speed) (Nindl et al., 2015).

Some researchers also have investigated a dispositional aspect of physical fitness, which reflects the degree to which individuals enjoy engaging in physical activity and are motivated to do so (Drasgow et al., 2012; Legree, Kilcullen, Putka, and Wasko, 2014).

Association with Performance

A number of studies have consistently found a relationship between physical fitness and leadership performance in the military academies. Rice et al. (1984) found a significant positive relationship between a U.S. Military Academy cadet's physical aptitude test[1] and leadership ratings during summer training. Atwater and Yammarino (1993) reported that leaders' athletic participation was the best predictor of follower ratings of transformational leadership at the U.S. Naval Academy. Atwater et al. (1999) followed 236 male cadets over four years and found that physical fitness significantly predicted both leadership emergence and leadership effectiveness.[2,3] These authors posit that physical fitness in this context is most likely acting as a proxy measure for other attributes important to leadership. In support of this idea, physical fitness was positively associated with self-esteem, hardiness, and conscientiousness (see also Hogan, 1989). Atwater and colleagues concluded that physical fitness is representative of mental strengths, as well as physical strengths, integral to leadership effectiveness and emergence. Related to this perspective, Brown (1991; 1988) suggests that physical fitness acts as a buffer to stressors, reducing adverse effects of stress over time and increasing the rate of recovery from stressors (cf. Robson, 2013).

---

[1] The physical aptitude test was administered to Academy applicants while still in high school (including tasks such as broad jump, basketball throw, and pull-ups).

[2] Physical fitness was measured through three fitness tests: pull-ups, sit-ups, and 1.5 mile run. Leadership emergence was measured by the rank obtained and leadership effectiveness was based on peer rankings collected in the fourth year.

[3] Prior influence experiences (i.e., life history data) also predicted leadership emergence and effectiveness.

Studies of military personnel have also examined dispositional aspects of physical fitness. In a meta-analysis (three studies comprising 5,995 individuals), Drasgow et al. (2012) found a small correlation between a dispositional measure of physical fitness and leadership effectiveness. More recently, Legree, Kilcullen, Putka, and Wasko (2014) examined a large set of variables, including Big Five facets and other characteristics related to temperament, as predictors of four measures of leader performance and potential among cadets. They found that dispositional measures of physical fitness predicted all four leadership criteria. In fact, the dispositional aspects of physical conditioning were the most important predictors across the four criteria.

Examining performance more generally, Nye et al. (2012) revealed a similar association of dispositional measures of physical fitness and performance ratings for enlisted personnel. Physical conditioning also is positively related to contextual performance (behaviors and activities such as helping and teamwork) and adaptability and negatively related to turnover and training failure (Drasgow et al., 2012; Nye et al., 2012).

Malleability

Meta-analysis and research reviews show that aspects of physical fitness, such as muscular strength, power, aerobic fitness, speed, body composition, balance, and coordination, are quite malleable (Courtright et al., 2013; Kraemer, Ratamess, and French, 2002; North Atlantic Treaty Organization Research and Technology Organization, 2009; Sharp, 1993). As these studies make clear, improvement depends on individuals' initial levels of fitness and characteristics of training programs, such as types of exercises or activities and duration of training. We note, however, that the term "training" when applied to physical fitness typically does not refer to formal training and education; instead, it corresponds more closely to "practice."

Measurement Tools

Given its many components, multiple performance tests would be required to measure the full spectrum of physical fitness. There are numerous tests to assess components of physical fitness (e.g., Knapik, et al., 2006; Nindl et al., 2015). Nindl et al. (2015) provide a list of field-expedient options (e.g., pull-up for muscular strength; standing broad jump for power, 40-yard sprint for speed; squat-thrusts for muscular endurance and coordination).

For decades, the Army has evaluated fitness using the Army Physical Fitness Test (APFT), which assesses muscular endurance and aerobic fitness. As described in Army FM 7-22, the AFPT consists of three tests: push-ups, sit-ups, and a two-mile run (Headquarters, Department of the Army, 2012a). All soldiers are required to take the APFT regularly, and scoring is age and gender-specific. In fiscal year 2017, the Army expects to implement a new set of physical fitness tests to evaluate recruits: the Occupational Physical Assessment Test (OPAT) (Vergun, 2017). The OPAT is gender-neutral and military occupational specialty–specific. It consists of the standing long jump, a seated power throw, a strength deadlift, and an interval aerobic measuring upper- and lower-body power, lower-body strength, and aerobic capacity.

The TAPAS, a personality assessment described previously in this report, includes a dispositional aspect of physical fitness called *physical conditioning*. Individuals with high scores on physical conditioning are likely to exercise and engage in physical activities. Examples of physical conditioning items on the TAPAS are "I like to exercise" and "I don't consider myself to be an athletic person" (reverse scored). Studies indicate that the association between the TAPAS' physical conditioning and APFT is moderate (Nye et al., 2012).

Generalized Self-Efficacy

Definition

Self-efficacy is the belief that one can execute a course of action in a particular situation (Bandura, 1982). Generalized self-efficacy (GSE) reflects an individual's perception of and belief in his or her ability to be successful across a variety of situations (e.g., Bandura, Adams, Hardy, and Howell, 1980).

Association with Performance

Foti and Hauenstein (2007) studied the association of GSE and other competencies with leadership outcomes among college freshmen of the Corps of Cadets, a militarily-structured organization at a university in the southeastern United States. The study showed that cadets with high scores on a set of individual characteristics consisting of GSE, measures of general cognitive ability, dominance, and self-monitoring, were more likely to emerge as leaders, to be promoted to other leadership positions, and to be rated as effective by their superiors than were cadets who had low or mixed ratings on the set of characteristics.

Judge and Bono (2001) conducted a meta-analysis of the association of GSE (as well as other core self-evaluation traits: self-esteem, locus of control, and emotional stability) with job performance more generally. The meta-analysis showed a small to moderate correlation of GSE and job performance across studies. This result is comparable to findings regarding the association of conscientiousness and job performance reported by Barrick and Mount (1991), which are discussed in Chapter Four of this report.

Malleability

Empirical studies have provided a convincing body of evidence that self-efficacy in relation to a specific task (i.e., specific self-efficacy) can be enhanced through training (e.g., Colquitt, LePine, and Noe, 2000; Schmidt and Ford, 2003). However, building self-efficacy within a specific domain may not necessarily extend across domains to all other areas; i.e., high specific self-efficacy does not necessarily mean high GSE (Sherer et al., 1982).

Researchers have viewed GSE as a stable, personality-like variable (Bandura, 1977; Chen et al., 2000; Harrison, Chadwick, and Scales, 1996). However, in contrast to a static personality trait that is not susceptible to change, scholars view GSE as dynamic (Bandura, 1999; cited in Mencl et al., 2012). Successful experiences within specific domains will eventually enhance individuals' self-efficacy more generally (Chen, Gully, and Eden, 2001). Bandura and colleagues showed that as people became more efficacious at specific tasks, their efficacy beliefs generalized more broadly to behaviors and tasks unrelated to their domain of expertise (e.g., Bandura, Adams, Hardy, and Howells, 1980). Thus, as several empirical studies now have shown, GSE is somewhat malleable (see also Eden and Aviram, 1993; Mencl et al., 2012; Schwoerer et al., 2005). These findings suggest that increases in GSE are unlikely to occur in response to a single training intervention but would accrue incrementally as a result of repeated successful performance on a diverse range of tasks.

Measurement Tools

Self-efficacy is measured with self-report scales (see Table 3.1). The New Generalized Self-Efficacy Scale (NGSE) (Chen, Gully, and Eden, 2001) is commonly used in research. Chen, Gully, and Eden (2001) developed this scale to address apparent psychometric issues with the Sherer et al. (1982) General Self-Efficacy (GSE) scale, which was the predominant measure at the time. Other commonly-used scales include the GSE subscale of the Self-Efficacy Scale (Sherer et al., 1982), and the General Perceived Self-Efficacy Scale (GPSE) (Schwarzer and Jerusalem, 1995), although there is evidence that the NGSE scale has stronger psychometric properties and is more efficient to administer (i.e., it uses fewer items) (Scherbaum, Cohen-Charash, and Kern, 2006).

Extraversion

Definition

Extraversion is one of the Big Five factors. Extraversion reflects tendencies to be sociable, dominant, active, and attention seeking. Numerous scholars have identified two major components of extraversion, one reflecting social dominance (also called potency or agency) and the other reflecting sociability or affiliation (e.g., see Judge et al., 2002; Roberts, Walton, and Viechtbauer, 2006). Lower-order facets of social dominance—which include dominance, independence, and self-confidence—are related to the concept of confidence in the ALRM.

Association with Performance

Numerous studies have examined the association of extraversion with leadership. Meta-analysis demonstrated that extraversion consistently

Table 3.1
Examples of Measures of Generalized Self-Efficacy

Measure	Description	Example items
NGSE (Chen, Gully, and Eden, 2001)	Eight items rated on five-point scales ranging from 1 = "strongly disagree" to 5 = "strongly agree"	• "I will be able to achieve most of the goals I have set for myself" • "Even when things are tough, I can perform quite well"
GSE subscale of the Self-Efficacy scale (Sherer et al., 1982)	Seventeen items rated on 14-point scales ranging from strongly disagree" to "strongly agree"	• "When I make plans, I am certain I can make them work" • "If I can't do a job the first time, I keep trying until I can" • "I avoid facing difficulties" (reverse scored)
GPSE (Schwarzer and Jerusalem, 1995)	Ten items rated on four-point scales ranging from 1 = "hardly true" to 4 = "exactly true"	• "Thanks to my resourcefulness, I can handle unforeseen situations" • "No matter what comes my way, I am usually able to handle it"

predicts leader outcomes (Judge et al., 2002). Judge and his colleagues found that among the Big Five factors, extraversion was the most consistent predictor of leadership across study settings (business, government or military, and student settings) and criteria, (i.e., leader emergence and leader effectiveness). Both the dominance and sociability facets were related to leadership. More recently, Do and Minbashian (2014) found that the social dominance component of extraversion was associated with both transformational leadership and leader effectiveness, whereas the affiliative component was not (and was negatively related to leader effectiveness). Do and Minbashian speculate that their results differ from other findings (e.g., Judge et al., 2002) because their analysis of each component of extraversion controls for the other component; this type of analysis was not possible in the Judge et al. (2002) study.

Other meta-analyses show that extraversion predicts job performance in occupations requiring social interaction (Barrick and Mount, 1991; Judge and Zapata, 2015) as well as in jobs involving higher competitive pressures and dealing with unpleasant or angry people (Judge and Zapata, 2015).

Malleability

In the meta-analysis of longitudinal changes in the Big Five discussed earlier, Roberts, Walton, and Viechtbauer (2006) found that the affiliative aspects of extraversion increased only in the 18 to 22 age group. Social dominance facets—which are associated with confidence—increased significantly in adolescence and in the college (ages 18 to 22) and young adulthood (ages 22 to 30 and 30 to 40) age groups. Individuals over 40 showed no change in social dominance. Roberts, Walton, and Viechtbauer (2006) posit that environmental factors, i.e., "universal tasks of social living" (p. 19), partly explain these increases, citing other research showing increases in self-confidence and dominance as individuals assume new social roles and experience occupational success (Clausen and Gilens, 1990; Roberts, 1997; Roberts, Caspi, and Moffitt, 2003; cf. Roberts, Walton, and Viechtbauer, 2006). That is, expectations that individuals encounter as they assume these new roles, coupled with consequences (rewards and punishments) that ensue from meeting or failing to meet these expectations, facilitate changes in social dominance.

Pursuing a military career corresponds to these changes in role demands. Thus, we might expect that career experiences and role demands in the Army foster development of the social dominance aspects of extraversion. This question could be examined in future research by investigating whether assigning personnel to roles with increased responsibility results in greater social dominance. Although training and education are part of these experiences, we would not expect the content of training and education efforts to have a direct effect on changes in extraversion.

Measurement Tools

Self-report instruments assessing the Big Five factors, as described earlier, provide measures of extraversion.

Resilience

Definition

The ALRM defines resilience as "the psychological and physical capacity to bounce back from life's stressors repeatedly to thrive in an era of high operational tempo" (Headquarters, Department of the Army, 2012b, p. 4-1). Matthews (2014) also suggests that resilience is, in part, the ability for an individual to turn trauma or adversity into positive growth. That is, when one learns from an adverse experience, the effect of subsequent trauma is diminished, and the individual's capacity to perform optimally increases. Bonanno (2004) reports that resilience is a commonly held trait with distinct pathways that individuals take in response to loss or trauma. Bonanno (2004) posits four pathways to resilience: hardiness, self-enhancement, repressive coping, and positive emotion and laughter. *Hardiness* is one of the more prominently studied pathways (Bartone et al., 2009; Maddi et al., 2010). According to Kobasa (1979), hardy people believe they have control over events in their lives, have a strong sense of commitment to life's activities, and view change as an exciting challenge in life. Notably, hardy people perceive stressful or painful experiences as a normal, interesting, and worthwhile part of life (Bartone, 2006).

Scholars have proposed other psychological constructs associated with resilience. *Dispositional optimism* is a trait that influences individuals' outcome expectations (i.e., whether they expect to be successful in the face of difficulties) and resulting behavior (i.e., whether the individuals respond by increasing or reducing their levels of effort) (Scheier and Carver, 1985). *Grit* (Duckworth et al., 2007) reflects passion for long-term goals and perseverance in the face of challenges.

Association with Performance

Hardiness has been associated with leader performance of military cadets in both field and academic settings (Bartone, Kelly, and Matthews, 2009). Bartone et al. (2013) found that the commitment and control facets of hardiness positively predicted leader performance grades at West Point, although effects were relatively modest. However, the control facet of hardiness strongly predicted adaptive performance as assessed by cadets' supervisors three years after graduation (when most graduates were first lieutenants). Bartone (2006) posits that hardiness is also important to leadership in that leaders influence the hardiness of their teams by serving as a role model, exemplifying "hardy" behaviors and responses, and by influencing team sense-making of events, e.g., by facilitating a positive construction of events and experiences and focusing on how the team can learn from its experiences.

Regarding performance more generally, research has shown that hardiness predicts responses to stress in a wide range of circumstances and settings, such as competitive sports, firefighting, corporate upheavals, military training and education, and other work and educational situations (see Maddi, 2007, for a review).

Much of the research on dispositional optimism has been in the context of health care, examining the effect of optimism on responses to health crises or on other health behaviors and outcomes. However, research has also examined the effect of dispositional optimism on goal attainment in other contexts, which has implications for job performance. For example, Geers, Wellman, and Lassiter (2009) conducted a series of studies of goal attainment among undergraduates in a range of domains (e.g., exercise persistence, scholastic achievement). Geers and his colleagues found a positive association between dispositional optimism and goal attainment when students rated the goals as having high priority. There also is evidence that optimism and other positive emotions enhance resilience or mediate the effect of resilience on responses to negative events (Fredrickson and Joiner, 2002; Fredrickson, Tugade, Waugh, and Larkin, 2003; Tugade, Fredrickson, and Barrett, 2004).

Research on grit shows that it is predictive of a range of outcomes for adults, such as educational attainment, grade point average at an elite university, completion of a rigorous summer training program (West Point), and first-year retention and graduation from West Point (Duckworth et al., 2007; Duckworth and Quinn, 2009; Kelly, Matthews, and Bartone, 2014; Maddi et al., 2012).

Malleability

There is some debate in the literature regarding the malleability of resilience. Hardiness was initially posited to be a dispositional trait that is learned early in life and is relatively stable over time (e.g., Kobasa, 1979; Kobasa, Maddi, and Kahn, 1982). Later work by Maddi and his colleagues, however, refer to hardiness as a set of attitudes and skills (e.g., Maddi, 2007). Dispositional optimism is also viewed as a personality trait that is influenced by heredity and childhood experiences and is relatively stable over time (see Carver, Scheier, and Segerstrom, 2010, for a review).

In relation to resilience and other positive constructs, such as hope and optimism, Wright (2007) proposed a continuum of stability. This proposition builds on theory and empirical evidence that these constructs may have some stability over time but are expected to be less stable than traits. Therefore, they are *state-like* and are subject to some change and development (e.g., Bandura, 1997; Carver and Scheier, 2005; Seligman, 1998; Snyder, 2000).

Both theory and empirical research support the notion that resilience can be developed through training. For example, Luthans, Avey, and Patera (2008) found that a relatively brief intervention (two, 45-minute online sessions conducted one week apart) produced improved psychological capital (a measure consisting of resilience, hope, optimism, and efficacy) compared to a control group. More recently, Johnson et al. (2014) showed that mechanisms related to stress recovery could be modified in healthy individuals prior to exposure to stress. They examined the effects of eight weeks of Mindfulness-Based Mind Fitness Training (MMFT) on resilience mechanisms in active-duty Marines preparing for deployment. MMFT emphasized internal awareness, attentional control, and sustained focus on present-moment experiences. The rates of stress recovery of participating Marines were measured by a variety of physiological indicators, which consistently revealed that those who received MMFT recovered from stress faster. After conducting a thorough overview of a medical database for the effects of various meditation techniques on resilience, Rees (2011) also found positive effects of meditation in general, and mindfulness in particular, on soldier resilience.

The Resilience Training Program (formerly, Battlemind Training), part of the Army's Comprehensive Soldier Fitness program, was also effective in reducing post-deployment adjustment problems among military personnel. In a randomized trial, Adler, Castro, and McGurk (2009) found that participants in Battlemind training or Battlemind debriefing reported fewer mental health symptoms at four-month follow-up (but only for those who had higher levels of combat exposure) compared to participants in a general stress education condition. In a similar vein, Griffith and West (2013) showed that, as a result of Master Resilience Training offered to Army National Guard, soldiers reported greater self-awareness and strength of character, including improved optimism, mental agility, and connection with others. There is some evidence, however, that training resilience during deployment may be less effective. In an evaluation of a 12-week resilience training program for soldiers deployed to Afghanistan, both resilient thinking and morale were observed to decline from the beginning to the end of training (Carr et al., 2013).

Measurement Tools

There are a large number of self-report scales measuring resilience or related constructs. Table 3.2 presents a sample of instruments used in numerous empirical studies.

The first two measures in Table 3.2, the PVS and DRS, are commercial measures of hardiness. Both scales have been used in studies of military personnel (e.g., Maddi et al., 2010; Bartone et al., 2008; Bartone et al., 2009; Bartone, Kelly, and Matthews, 2013; Kelly, Matthews, and Bartone, 2014). The Grit Scale has been used in a variety of domains, including military research (Kelly, Matthews, and Bartone, 2014; Maddi et al., 2012). The LOT (Scheier and Carver, 1985; Scheier, Carver, and Bridges, 1994) and LOT-R (Carver, 2013), which measure dispositional optimism, are included here in light of research showing associations of dispositional optimism with responses to stress.

Presence: Summary of Findings

Table 3.3 summarizes findings regarding the malleability and measurement of constructs associated with presence.

Table 3.2
Examples of Resilience Measures

Measure	Description	Example items
Personal Views Survey (PVS) III-R (Maddi et al., 2009)	Commercial instrument consisting of 18 items measuring three aspects of hardiness: control, commitment, and challenge. Uses four-point rating scales regarding relevance to the respondent.	• "Changes in routine provoke me to learn" • "I am not equipped to handle the unexpected problems of life" (reverse scored)
Dispositional Resilience Scale (DRS)-15; (Bartone, 1995; 2007)	Based on the PVS, the DRS-15 is a commercial instrument consisting of 15 items addressing commitment, control, and challenge rated on four-point scales ranging from "not at all true" to "completely true."	• "Most of my life gets spent doing things that are worthwhile" • "Planning ahead can help avoid most future problem"
The Grit Scale (Duckworth et al., 2007; Duckworth and Quinn, 2009)	12-item and eight-item scales consist of two subscales: perseverance and consistency of interests. Items have five-point response options ranging from "Very much like me" to "Not like me at all."	• "I finish whatever I begin" (perseverance) • "New ideas and projects sometimes distract me from previous ones" (consistency of interests; reverse scored)
Life Orientation Test (LOT); (Scheier and Carver, 1985; Scheier, Carver, and Bridges, 1994), and LOT-revised (LOT-R) (Carver, 2013)	The LOT measures dispositional optimism using eight items plus four filler items, rated on five-point scales ranging from "strongly disagree" to "strongly agree." LOT-R consists of six items plus four filler items with five-point response options ranging from "I agree a lot" to "I disagree a lot."	• "In uncertain times, I usually expect the best" • "I hardly ever expect things to go my way" (reverse scored)

Table 3.3
Summary of Research on Malleability and Common Measures: Presence

Construct	Malleability	Common Measures
Physical fitness	Highly malleable, particularly with appropriate physical training programs.	APFT
Generalized self-efficacy	Considered a "dynamic" (rather than static) personality trait that is somewhat malleable and will increase over time and with successful experiences in different domains. This suggests that success in training could contribute to GSE indirectly.	Self-report measures including the New Generalized Self-Efficacy scale (Chen, Gully, and Eden, 2001), the Generalized Self-Efficacy scale (Sherer et al., 1982), and General Self-Efficacy subscale of the Self-Efficacy scale (Schwarzer and Jerusalem, 1995)
Extraversion	Research evidence suggests that training will not have direct effects on extraversion. Studies of personality traits across the lifespan show increases in social dominance up to age 40. Changes are thought to occur in response to shifting role demands and expectations; therefore, work experiences may bring about changes in social dominance.	Self-report measures as discussed in Chapter Two, e.g., TAPAS (Drasgow et al., 2012), IPIP (Goldberg, 1999), NEO PI-R (Costa and McCrae, 1992), and HPI (Hogan and Hogan, 1995)
Resilience	Studies of resiliency training programs show that resilience can be developed or enhanced.	Self-report measures including the Personal Views Survey III-R (Maddi et al., 2009) and Dispositional Resilience Scale (Bartone, 1995, 2007) Measures of related constructs include the Grit Scale (Duckworth et al., 2007; Duckworth and Quinn, 2009) and the Life Orientation Test (Scheier and Carver, 1985; Scheier, Carver, and Bridges, 1994) and LOT-Revised (Carver, 2013)

CHAPTER FOUR

Character

The ALRM conceives of *character* as the set of an individual's morals and ethics; character helps leaders distinguish right from wrong and to make the right choices in difficult situations (Headquarters, Department of the Army, 2012b).

Constructs from theoretical and empirical literature related to character include ethical decisionmaking, initiative, conscientiousness, motivation to lead, and affective commitment. As in previous chapters, Chapter Four is organized according to the constructs. We present definitions, discuss the findings about association of the constructs with leadership and general job performance or related outcomes, review findings related to the malleability of the construct, and present specific measurements. We summarize the findings in Table 4.3.

Ethical Decisionmaking

Definition

A definition of ethical decisionmaking is somewhat elusive because scholars are often hesitant to define what is ethical or moral (Tenbrunsel and Smith-Crowe, 2008). Jones (1991) suggests, "an ethical decision is a decision that is both legally and morally acceptable to the larger community" (p. 367). Similarly, Treviño, Weaver, and Reynolds (2006) state, "behavioral ethics refers to individual behavior that is subject to or judged according to generally accepted moral norms of behavior" (p. 952).[1]

Individual-level ethical decisionmaking can be divided into two primary streams of research. One assumes a rational and deliberate, step-by-step process, and the other incorporates a more affective approach. Perhaps the most cited rational model is that of Kohlberg (1969), who proposed a stage theory of cognitive moral development to explain how people think about interacting with their social environment.[2] The affective approach suggests more automatic responses to ethical issues, which can involve an instantaneous judgment of right and wrong, with rationalization of the judgment occurring later (e.g., Haidt, 2001; Reynolds, 2006; Sonenshein, 2007).

There is an enormous literature on ethical decisionmaking and related concepts such as moral thinking and behavior that spans a range of disciplines (e.g., psychology, philosophy, management, political science, history, theology), domains (e.g., business ethics, medical ethics, ethics in scientific research), and predictors (e.g., age, gender, work experience, profession, organizational culture, rewards, nationality). A review of this work is beyond the scope of this report; therefore, we focus on review papers and seminal articles addressing leadership. Interestingly,

---

[1] Treviño, den Nieuwenboer, and Kish-Gephart (2014) describe three related perspectives of how to consider what is ethical: "unethical behavior that is contrary to accepted moral norms in society (e.g., lying, cheating, stealing); routine ethical behavior that meets the minimum moral standards of society (e.g., honesty, treating people with respect); and extraordinary ethical behavior that goes beyond society's moral minima (e.g., charitable giving, whistleblowing)" (pp. 636–637).

[2] Another rational model that has been the subject of a great deal of subsequent research (Rest, 1986a; cited in O'Fallon and Butterfield, 2005) proposes that ethical decisionmaking occurs in four steps: (1) moral awareness (identifying that an issue entails ethical significance); (2) moral judgment (the process of deciding what is right or wrong); (3) forming an intention to act; and (4) taking action. Rest, Narvaez, Bebeau, and Thoma (1999) later proposed three schemas of moral reasoning that are ordered developmentally and proceed from least to most advanced. The schemas consist of: (1) personal interest, which is based on a preference for self-serving moral thinking without consideration to larger social systems; (2) maintaining norms, representative of a society-wide moral perspective, which emphasizes rules, roles, and authorities; and (3) postconventional thinking, in which moral obligations are based on shared ideals and community experiences, are reciprocal, and are open to discussion and examination.

we found only a small number of papers addressing moral reasoning and decisionmaking in military contexts (Atwater et al., 1998; 1999; Olsen, Eid, and Johnsen, 2006).

Association with Performance

Although there are meta-analyses or reviews on ethical climate (Martin and Cullen, 2006), whistleblowing (Mesmer-Magnus and Viswesvaran, 2005), and the antecedents to ethical decisionmaking and related concepts such as moral awareness, judgment, and intentions (Kish-Gephart, Harrison, and Treviño, 2010; O'Fallon and Butterfield, 2005), we did not find any quantitative reviews for ethical decisionmaking and performance. Some primary studies have shown positive effects of ethical behavior in organizations, although findings are mixed. Much of the research has focused on moral judgment or reasoning, particularly on post-conventional thinking, the most advanced stage or type of moral reasoning (Kohlberg, 1969; Rest et al., 1999).[3] Across sample types (civilian and cadets),[4] post-conventional thinking is positively associated with transformational leadership behaviors (Olsen, Eid, and Johnsen, 2006; Turner et al., 2002), and ratings of performance by managers' superiors (Sosik, Juzbasich, and Chun, 2011) but not with transactional leadership (Sosik, Juzbasich, and Chun, 2011).[5] However, in a longitudinal study of Army cadets, moral reasoning was not associated with leader emergence or effectiveness (Atwater et al., 1999). In a study examining punishment (which is an aspect of transactional leadership),

---

[3] Rest et al. (1999) found evidence for three schemas of increasingly complex moral reasoning: (1) personal interest, the most "primitive" schema, is based on the preference for self-serving moral thinking and no consideration is given to the larger social systems; (2) maintaining norms, representative of a society-wide moral perspective, is based on the importance of rules, roles, and authorities; and (3) postconventional thinking, the most advanced schema, suggests that moral obligations are based on shared ideals and community experiences, which are reciprocal and open to discussion and examination.

[4] Olsen, Eid, and Johnsen (2006) examined Norwegian naval officer cadets; Turner et al. (2002) and Sosik, Juzbasich, and Chun (2011) examined civilian managers; and Atwater and colleagues (1998; 1999) examined West Point cadets.

[5] See Brown and Treviño (2006) for a theoretical discussion about the association of ethical leadership and transformational leadership.

Atwater et al. (1998) found that moral reasoning was associated with the use of contingent punishment, but there was no difference between leaders with high and low moral reasoning in use of noncontingent punishment. Contingent punishment, in turn, was positively related to peer rankings of leadership effectiveness.[6]

More recently, Brown, Treviño, and Harrison (2005) examined the association of ethical leadership, specifically, with other outcomes. They found that ethical leadership was positively related to affective trust in leaders and negatively related to abusive supervision, and it predicted outcomes including followers' satisfaction with the leader, perceived leader effectiveness, dedication to their jobs, and willingness to report problems to management.

Malleability

Like other aspects of ethical behavior, there are many studies on the development of moral thinking and behavior (particularly in children) and on training these constructs in a wide range of domains (e.g., general education ranging from primary to postsecondary education, business, medicine, and research science) that exceed the scope of this report. Moreover, we have not found review papers or meta-analyses on this topic. Several papers have pointed to conflicting findings about the effectiveness of training to improve ethical thinking and behavior (e.g., Mumford et al., 2008; Seiler, Fischer, and Ooi, 2010). Some studies find positive effects; others find more limited or no effects, and some even find negative effects. Seiler and his colleagues attribute conflicting findings to differences in training duration and intensity, training content (e.g., complex cognitive processing versus intuitive processing), and differences in how moral decisionmaking is measured. Thus, the literature on the degree to which ethical thinking and behavior can be trained is inconclusive.

---

[6] Contingent punishment is punishment that is based on specific standards. Atwater et al. (1998) argue that contingency punishment is associated with leadership effectiveness in part because it is delivered in response to poor performance or unacceptable behavior with the intention of improving future performance, and because active styles of leadership are typically seen as more effective than passive styles.

Seiler, Fischer, and Ooi (2010) present a model of moral decision-making that incorporates both rational and intuitive processes. Seiler and his colleagues discuss the implications of the model for military training interventions.[7] For example, given that decisions are highly context-specific, training should focus not only on general principles of moral judgment but on situations of relevance to military decision-making. Other recommendations include the use of actual or realistic (rather than hypothetical) moral dilemmas; teaching problem-solving, critical thinking, and procedural strategies to encourage consideration of possible consequences of responses to moral dilemmas and to be aware of potential influences of cognitive biases on judgments; addressing how social influence can affect moral judgments; and use of practical exercises repeated over time and accompanied by feedback to develop patterns of moral thinking. Future work will need to examine the effectiveness of these recommendations for developing moral reasoning and behavior in military contexts.

Measurement Tools

Measures of moral thinking and behavior consist of interviews, SJTs, and surveys. Early measurement of moral reasoning relied on Kohlberg's (1969) semistructured interview to understand how people solve ethical dilemmas. However, the Defining Issues Test (DIT) (Rest, 1986b; Rest et al., 1999), an SJT that can be administered online or via paper and pencil, is the most widely used measure (e.g., Kish-Gephart, Harrison, and Treviño, 2010; see also Thoma, 2002, and Thoma, Narvaez, Rest, and Derryberry, 1999). There are two primary versions: DIT and DIT-2, where the DIT-2 is a shorter instrument with updated items. A respondent is presented with a dilemma (e.g., a father contemplates stealing food for his starving family) and first answers yes or no as to what he or she should do (e.g., report the father). Then the respondent is

[7] This model comprises five aspects: (a) moral perception, (b) internal dual-process (i.e., the individual experiences the internal processes of reasoning and intuition), (c) moral judgment and decision, (d) post hoc reasoning (to further support his/her judgment), and (e) social interaction (the individual interacts with others during and after the problem-solving process, which influences his or her internal dual process to reach a more nuanced or different moral judgment and decision).

asked to rate 12 considerations for determining the right choice on a scale from one (least important) to five (most important). Each of these considerations reflects issues distinct to the stages of cognitive moral development. Then, respondents are asked to rank the four most important arguments that influenced their yes or no decision.

More recently, Brown, Treviño, and Harrison (2005) developed a 10-item survey specific to leadership at the supervisory level, the Ethical Leadership Scale (ELS), which they validated in a series of studies. Examples of items include, "Listens to what employees have to say," "Can be trusted," and "Defines success not just by results but also the way that they are obtained."

Conscientiousness, which is one of the Big Five factors, includes a facet reflecting moral behavior. Conscientiousness is discussed in more detail later in this chapter. Measures of the Big Five factors were discussed in Chapter Two.

Initiative

Definition

Initiative is another aspect of Army values that has been addressed in research. Initiative is part of a broader construct called *active performance*, which includes concepts such as personal initiative, engagement, proactivity, taking charge, adaptive performance, helping behavior, and voice (Frese, 2008). These concepts reflect several common characteristics, such as being action oriented or a self-starter, having a change orientation, and being future-focused (e.g., anticipating problems) (Tornau and Frese, 2013). As described earlier in this report, several of these concepts and characteristics, along with behaviors such as setting difficult goals and engaging in extended practice, are also important for developing expertise (see, e.g., Ericsson, 2006; Phillips, Klein, and Sieck, 2004). However, as Tornau and Frese (2013) make clear in a recent review, theory and research methods often confound two related clusters of proactivity: one that reflects dispositional traits (proactive personality and personal initiative/personality) and the other, which reflects behaviors observable to others (taking charge, voice, and personal initiative/behavior). This distinction is important because it influences measurement and conclusions.

Association with Performance

We found limited research examining personal initiative and leadership. One exception is Crant and Bateman (2000), who found that proactive personality was positively associated with charismatic leadership.

Tornau and Frese (2013) conducted the most recent meta-analysis of personal initiative and job outcomes. Overall, personal initiative measures were associated with outcomes such as performance and innovation; interesting, objective outcome measures (e.g., sales, salary, business growth) had stronger correlations with behavioral measures of personal initiative and weaker correlations with dispositional measures. In addition, behavioral measures of personal initiative predicted job performance beyond the Big Five. Tornau and Frese (2013) also found that dispositional measures of personal initiative did not explain variance in objective performance beyond the Big Five. In particular, dispositional measures of personal initiative were strongly and positively correlated with extraversion and conscientiousness, and to a lesser extent, negatively correlated with agreeableness. These findings suggest that behavioral measures of initiative are preferable for predicting job performance.

Malleability

Research regarding the effects of training on initiative is primarily limited to unpublished dissertations (e.g., Bassyiouny, 2007; Garman, 2002; cf. Tornau and Frese, 2013; Glaub, 2009) with the one exception of one paper by Kirby, Kirby, and Lewis (2002). Therefore, the generalizability of these conclusions merits further investigation; however, we discuss one of these studies in further detail for possible insights. Glaub (2009) designed a three-day, theory-based, personal initiative training and examined its effectiveness through a randomized control group pretest/posttest design with business owners in Uganda. Data were collected at four time points: (1) before training; (2) directly after training; (3) approximately four to five months after training; and (4) 12 months after training. Study results showed promising long-term effects for objective outcomes (e.g., business success).

Findings from Tornau and Frese (2013) regarding the association of dispositional measures of personal initiative and the Big Five, coupled with findings discussed earlier about the malleability of Big Five factors such as extraversion and conscientiousness (Roberts, Walton, and Viechtbauer, 2006), suggest that personal initiative as a dispositional characteristic is unlikely to be changed via education and training, but it might be malleable through developmental job experiences. There is insufficient research to determine the malleability of behavioral aspects of personal initiative.

Measurement Tools

There are many instruments that rely on different methods (self-ratings, other-ratings, interviews, and SJTs) used to evaluate initiative. In line with the distinction between dispositional and behavioral measures of personal initiative, we review some measures from each perspective. Arguably, the most widely used measure to assess proactive personality is Bateman and Crant's (1993) self-report questionnaire. This is a dispositional, self-report measure consisting of 17 items; examples include, "I excel at identifying opportunities" and "No matter what the odds, if I believe in something, I will make it happen." Respondents provide answers using a seven-point scale ranging from strongly disagree to strongly agree.

As noted earlier, Tornau and Frese (2013) found that personal initiative was associated with conscientiousness and extraversion. We expect that initiative is closely related to social dominance facets of extraversion and the achievement orientation facets of conscientiousness. For example, individuals with high scores on the dominance facet of extraversion in the TAPAS are described as "take charge," and are often referred to by their peers as "natural leaders," and individuals with high scores on the achievement facet are considered "hard working, ambitious, confident, and resourceful" (Drasgow et al., 2012, p. 39). Instruments measuring the Big Five are discussed in Chapter Two of this report.

Table 4.1 describes several behavioral measures of initiative. The first two measures are "other reports" in which people (e.g., a coworker or supervisor) rate the target individual. The third measure consists of a structured interview designed to assess personal initiative. The fourth instrument is an SJT of personal initiative.

Table 4.1
Examples of Behavioral Measures of Initiative

Measure	Description	Examples
Extra-role behaviors (Van Dyne and LePine, 1998)	"Other-report" measure consisting of 13 items reflecting helping behaviors and voice (i.e., the propensity to speak up to promote change). Response options range from 1 = "strongly disagree" to 7 = "strongly agree."	• "This particular coworker volunteers to do things for this work group" (helping) • "This particular coworker speaks up and encourages others in this group to get involved in issues that affect the group" (voice)
Taking charge (Morrison and Phelps, 1999)	"Other-report" measure, consisting of 10 statements rated on a five-point scale from 1 = "strongly disagree" to 5 = "strongly agree."	• "This person often tries to institute new work methods that are more effective for the company" • "This person often tries to implement solutions to pressing organizational problems"
Interview of personal initiative (Frese et al., 1997; Frese, Kring, Soose, and Zempel, 1996)	Structured interview to measure facets of personal initiative such as proactivity and overcoming barriers. Interviewers rate responses (e.g., for demonstration of initiative) using five-point scales, and they document factual information, such as the respondent's employment status.	• "Have you changed something in your work during the last year" (e.g., the sequence of activities, added other activities, etc.)? • "Pretend for a moment that you are dismissed from your job. What will you do?"
SJT of personal initiative (Bledow and Frese, 2009)	Consists of 12 common scenarios requiring personal initiative in the workplace. Each scenario has four or five response options; respondents select the options they mostly like and least likely to perform.	Examples include scenarios in which (1) a new program was installed on computers in your department and no training was provided, and (2) conflict among other colleagues is creating tension in your department.

Conscientiousness

Definition

Conscientiousness is a Big Five factor that is defined in terms of multiple facets. Several researchers discuss two higher-order facets corresponding to achievement (also called industriousness or proactive aspects) and dependability (also called reliability, responsibility, or inhibitive aspects) (see Roberts et al., 2005, for a review). Roberts et al. (2005) identified six lower-order facets: industriousness, order, self-control, responsibility, traditionalism, and virtue.[8] Most of these facets map on to one or more of the ALRM attributes. Proactive facets of conscientiousness, like industriousness and order, are associated with personal initiative in the ALRM; virtue is associated with Army values, such as honor and integrity; responsibility is associated with values of duty and selfless service; and self-control, order, and traditionalism are associated with discipline as defined in the ALRM.

Association with Performance

The association of conscientiousness with leader and job performance is well documented. Unless noted, most studies measure conscientiousness as a single or unidimensional construct, rather than measuring lower-order facets.

In their meta-analysis of the Big Five factors and leadership, Judge et al. (2002) showed that extraversion, followed by conscientiousness, had the highest correlations with leadership. In multivariate analyses (which included all five factors), conscientiousness was the strongest predictor of leader emergence and overall leadership, but it did not predict leader effectiveness.

Barrick and Mount (1991) conducted a meta-analysis of the Big Five factors and three job performance criteria (job proficiency, training proficiency, and personnel data, e.g., salary, tenure, and turnover) and five occupational groups; they found that conscientiousness was associated with all three criteria for all groups. In their recent meta-analysis, Judge and Zapata (2015) found a strong correlation between

---

[8] Roberts et al. (2005) describe the six facets as follows. Industriousness is associated with being hardworking, ambitious, confidence, and resourceful. Order is associated with planning and organizing activities and tasks. Self-control is associated with being cautious, level-headed, patient, and able to delay gratification. Responsibility is associated with being cooperative, dependable, and providing service to others. Traditionalism is associated with being compliant with rules and expectations. Virtue is associated with adherence to standards of honesty and morality.

conscientiousness and job performance for two types of jobs: jobs in which individuals have freedom to determine how to perform their work, and jobs requiring independence. However, in contrast to predictions, the association between conscientiousness and performance in jobs requiring attention to detail was negative (Judge and Zapata, 2015). Follow-up analysis to this surprising finding suggests that the achievement and dependability aspects of conscientiousness may be counteracting one another. Specifically, achievement orientation was negatively related to performance in jobs requiring attention to detail, whereas dependability was positively related. Judge and Zapata (2015) hypothesize that dependability is more relevant to jobs requiring attention to detail, whereas individuals who are achievement oriented might be frustrated in these jobs. The reason conscientiousness, overall, showed a negative relationship with job performance in jobs requiring attention to detail is because there were more studies assessing achievement orientation.

Malleability

The meta-analysis of change in the Big Five factors across the lifespan described earlier (Roberts, Walton, and Viechtbauer, 2006) showed little change in conscientiousness in adolescence and in college-age individuals (ages 18 to 22) but significant increases among young adults ages 22 to 30 as well as in subsequent decades until age 70. As noted in the discussion of extraversion earlier in this report, Roberts, Walton, and Viechtbauer (2006) conclude that these changes may occur in response to life experiences and lessons learned due to changing role demands. Thus, while the Army might be able to influence conscientiousness early in soldiers' careers via job assignments, we would not expect that education or training content would lead to changes in conscientiousness.

Measurement Tools

Self-report instruments assessing the Big Five factors as described earlier, provide measures of conscientiousness. Several Big Five instruments measure facets of the factors, but only the TAPAS measures all six lower-order facets of conscientiousness as identified by Roberts and colleagues (2005).

Motivation to Lead

Definition

Motivation to lead (MTL) is a construct developed by Chan and Drasgow (2001), which they define as a characteristic that influences a leader's or future leader's "decisions to assume leadership training, roles, and responsibilities and that affect his or her intensity of effort at leading and persistence as a leader" (p. 482). Thus, MTL appears to map onto the "internal shared attitudes and beliefs that embody the spirit of the Army profession" element of warrior ethos and service ethos in the ALRM (Headquarters, Department of the Army, 2012b, p. 4-2). Chan and Drasgow conceptualized MTL as consisting of three, related dimensions: affective-identity, which reflects enjoyment of being a leader; social-normative, which reflects a sense of duty to lead; and noncalculative, which reflects not being concerned about the costs associated with the responsibilities of being a leader relative to its benefits.

Association with Performance

The importance of MTL has begun to accumulate a substantial amount of theoretical attention (e.g., DeRue and Ashford, 2010; Epitropaki, Kark, Mainemelis, and Lord, 2016; Kark and Van Dijk, 2007). In addition, several primary studies have shown that MTL is associated with leadership potential or outcomes. Chan and Drasgow (2001) examined the association of MTL with leader potential in three samples (Singapore military recruits, Singapore junior college students, and U.S. undergraduate students). The study found that the affective-identity and noncalculative MTL predicted leader potential beyond other variables such as GMA and Big Five factors. Social-normative MTL was correlated with leader potential, but unlike the other dimensions of MTL, did not predict the outcome beyond the other variables in the model. In subsequent research, Amit, Lisak, Popper, and Gal (2007) showed that all three dimensions of MTL distinguished leaders from nonleaders among soldiers in the Israeli Defense Forces. In a study of college students, Hong, Catano, and Liao (2011) found that the affective-identity component of MTL predicted leader emergence in group problem-solving discussions, and the social normative component predicted assuming leadership roles in long-term projects. Finally, using a biodata measure of dispositional traits, Legree, Kilcullen, Putka, and Wasko (2014) found that interest in being a leader predicted leader effectiveness and potential among ROTC cadets.

Malleability

There is little research on the degree to which MTL can be developed through formal training. Although past theories consider leadership motivation constructs as stable individual differences, Chan and Drasgow's (2001) note that there has been considerable controversy or methodological concerns about measures of these concepts. Chan and Drasgow propose that MTL is malleable, at least in part, and is influenced by both stable personality traits and job experience. Their research supported these predictions; antecedents of MTL included more stable traits, such as Big Five factors, and past leadership experience.

From a lifespan perspective, in a longitudinal study that followed study participants from childhood to young adulthood, Gottfried et al. (2011) found that children who had higher intrinsic academic motivation, i.e., who enjoy learning for its own sake, showed higher affective-identify and noncalculative MTL in young adulthood. This was particularly the case when leadership tasks involved facing challenging and novel situations. Gottfried and her colleagues concluded that childrearing practices that foster academic motivation have subsequent effects on leadership. These findings suggest that MTL is malleable but we would not expect it to change via training and education for adults.

Measurement Tools

Chan and Drasgow (2001) developed and tested a 27-item self-report measure of MTL used in their original research and the subsequent studies described earlier. Examples of items include "Most of the time, I prefer being a leader rather than a follower when working in a group" (affective-identity MTL), "If I agree to lead a group, I would never expect any advantages or special benefits" (noncalculative MTL), and "I feel that I have a duty to lead others if I am asked" (social-normative MTL). This instrument has also been used in subsequent research on MTL (e.g., Amit, Lisak, Popper, and Gal, 2007; Hong, Catano, and Liao, 2011; Gottfried et al., 2011).

Affective Commitment

Definition

Affective commitment is defined as an employee's emotional attachment to, identification with, and involvement in the organization (Allen and Meyer, 1990). This construct appears to map onto soldiers' and civilians' "commitment to the nation, mission, unit, and fellow soldiers" element of the warrior ethos and service ethos attribute in the ALRM (Headquarters, Department of the Army, 2012b, p. 4-2).

According to the seminal three-component model of organizational commitment proposed by Allen and Meyer (1990), affective commitment is one of three forms of commitment. The other forms are continuance commitment (the perceived cost of leaving the organization) and normative commitment (feeling an obligation to stay). In 2003, a special issue of *Military Psychology* (Volume 15, Issue 3) presented a series of studies addressing organizational commitment in the military organized around Allen and Meyer's three-component model. Indeed, this theoretical model has been the dominant perspective of organizational commitment; however, empirical support has been mixed (Meyer, Stanley, Herscovitch, and Topolnytsky, 2002). Solinger, van Olffen, and Roe (2008) recommended a reconceptualization of organizational commitment such that it is best described as a general attitude toward the organization, whereas normative and continuance commitment are attitudes regarding specific behaviors (i.e., staying or leaving). We acknowledge these emerging theoretical developments; however, we focus on affective commitment, given the extensive research on this construct.

Association with Performance

With respect to leadership performance, affective commitment is typically construed as an outcome variable as opposed to a predictor variable. That is, there is a large body of research examining the relationship between various indicators of leaders' performance and followers' affective commitment (e.g., Gerstner and Day, 1997; Eisenberger et al., 2010). In contrast, the relationship between leaders' affective commitment and their own leadership performance is relatively unexplored. One notable exception is Karrasch (2003), who found a small positive relationship between affective commitment and Army captains' leadership performance as rated by their peers.

Expanding the performance domain from leadership to general job performance, however, reveals positive effects. Meta-analyses report a small to moderate positive relationship between affective commitment and job performance (Meyer et al., 2002; Riketta, 2002). Other correlates of affective commitment include organizational citizenship behaviors (behaviors that go above and beyond basic job requirements and benefit the organization), which also show a small to moderate positive relationship, and withdrawal behaviors such as absenteeism and turnover, which show small to moderate negative relationships (Meyer et al., 2002).

Malleability

Affective commitment is typically considered a job attitude (Schleicher, Hansen, and Fox, 2011). Research has identified many antecedents of this attitude, including characteristics of the person (e.g., locus of control) as well as aspects of the job and organization. Factors that influence affective commitment include perceptions of organizational and leader support, role clarity, and perceptions of fairness in the workplace (e.g., organizational justice and fulfillment of psychological contracts) (Dirks and Ferrin, 2002; Meyer et al., 2002; Zhao, Wayne, Glibkowski, and Bravo, 2007). These findings suggest that organizational practices, such as clarifying individual roles, can improve affective commitment. We would expect that opportunities for training and education might affect organizational commitment, but we would not expect the content of training and education to directly influence this construct.

Measurement Tools

The primary measures used to assess affective commitment are presented in Table 4.2. As can be seen by the example items, these scales focus on employee's emotional attachment to, identification with, and/or involvement in the organization. The Affective Commitment Questionnaire (ACQ) and Organizational Commitment Questionnaire (OCQ) are

Table 4.2
Examples of Affective Commitment Measures

Measure	Description	Example items
ACS (Allen and Meyer, 1990; Meyer, Allen, and Smith, 1993)	The original ACS measure consisted of eight items and the revised measure consisted of six items. Both use a seven-point rating scale ranging from "strongly disagree" to "strongly agree."	• "This organization has a great deal of personal meaning for me" • "I do not feel a strong sense of 'belonging' to my organization" (reverse scored)
OCQ (Mowday, Steers, and Porter, 1979)	Fifteen-item measure that uses a seven-point rating scale ranging from "strongly disagree" to "strongly agree."	• "I am proud to tell others that I am part of this organization" • "It would take very little change in my present circumstance to cause me to leave this organization" (reverse scored)
Identification/ Internalization Typology (O'Reilly and Chatman, 1986)	Five items represent identification and three items represent internalization. All items are evaluated on a seven-point rating scale ranging from "strongly disagree" to "strongly agree."	• "The reason I prefer this organization to others is because of what it stands for, its values" (identification) • "I feel a sense of 'ownership' for this organization rather than being just an employee" (internalization)

the most commonly used measures (as indicated by meta-analyses; e.g., Riketta, 2002).

Character: Summary of Findings

Table 4.3 presents three constructs that represent character and that have been the focus of empirical research.

Table 4.3
Summary of Research on Malleability and Common Measures: Character

Construct	Malleability	Common Measures
Ethical decisionmaking	Research findings conflict about development of ethical decisionmaking through training. It is likely that program characteristics affect the impact of training.	Defining Issues Test (DIT) (Rest, 1986b); DIT-2 (Rest et al., 1999); Ethical Leadership Scale (ELS) (Brown, Treviño, and Harrison, 2005)
Initiative	There is insufficient empirical literature to draw strong conclusions about the trainability of initiative.	Proactive personality scale (Bateman and Crant, 1993); personal initiative situational judgment test (Bledow and Frese, 2009)
Conscientiousness	We would not expect formal training and education to have a direct effect on conscientiousness, but changes in conscientiousness across the lifespan are thought to occur in response to shifting role demands and expectations, suggesting that job experiences might affect conscientiousness.	Self-report measures including facets in the TAPAS (Drasgow et al., 2012), NEO PI-R (Costa and McCrae, 1992), and HPI (Hogan and Hogan, 1995)
MTL	We would not expect formal training and education to have a direct effect on MTL, but some findings indicate that MTL can be developed through social learning and job experiences.	A self-report scale measuring MTL (Chan and Drasgow, 2001) has been used in a number of studies of leadership.
Affective commitment	Affective commitment is considered a job attitude that is influenced by organizational practices, such as clarifying individual roles and perceptions of fair treatment. We would not expect training and education to directly influence affective commitment.	Self-report measures include the Affective Commitment Questionnaire (Allen and Meyer, 1990; Meyer, Allen, and Smith, 1993); the Organizational Commitment Questionnaire (Mowday, Steers, and Porter, 1979); and Identification/Internalization Typology (O'Reilly and Chatman, 1986).

CHAPTER FIVE

Conclusions, Implications, and Future Directions

Today's volatile and complex operational environment has a profound effect on the qualities Army leaders must bring to their job. The Army has taken many steps to consider this environment in defining leadership qualities through policy, documents, and training related to the ALRM and the Army Human Dimension Strategy for 2015.

To help the Army reach its goals in preparing current and future leaders, this project sought to explore the degree in which leadership qualities can be taught and measured. We focused on the three categories of attributes presented by the ALRM: character, presence, and intellect. Because many of these attributes do not parallel those found in theoretical and empirical research, we first mapped the ALRM attributes to constructs associated with each attribute. We then reviewed the research for each of these constructs with respect to their associations with leader and job performance, malleability, including the "teach-ability" of each construct, and tools to measure these constructs.

In this chapter, we summarize the key findings regarding malleability and discuss how the Army might determine whether to focus efforts on soldier development or selection for ALRM attributes. We then address methodological questions regarding measurement, particularly to support the goal of investigating whether training and education bring about changes in leader characteristics. We present considerations about what methods of measurement to use, discuss selection of measures in terms of their content, and describe designs for studying training and education interventions and how design decisions affect the conclusions one can draw about the effects of the interventions. Following the discussion of methodological topics, we provide recommendations for routine measurement of key constructs in the Army at large. We conclude by addressing limitations of this literature review and proposing topics for future research.

What Constructs Can Be Developed Through Training and Education?

Like Mueller-Hanson et al. (2005), who reviewed characteristics associated with adaptability, we summarize the degree to which constructs associated with ALRM attributes can be developed through training and education by arraying them along a continuum ranging from less to more malleable (see Figure 5.1). We also note attributes that may be malleable through other means (work experiences or organizational practices) and attributes for which additional research is needed to draw conclusions about malleability.

As discussed in Chapter One, Mueller-Hanson et al. (2005) concluded that cognitive ability, resilience, and achievement motivation (which are facets of conscientiousness) are resistant to change via training. We concur with this conclusion for cognitive ability, i.e., GMA, and the affiliative facets of extraversion.[1] We also agree that conscientiousness is not likely to change as a result of training; however, evidence for changes in conscientiousness with shifts in role experiences in young adulthood (Roberts, Walton, and Viechtbauer, 2006) suggests that this Big Five dimension might be influenced by job assignments in the early stages of leaders' careers.

We draw somewhat different conclusions about other characteristics that Mueller-Hanson and her colleagues deemed resistant to change. Our review of the research indicates that, although changes in openness to experience are likely normative in nature, creative problem-solving

[1] We also agree with Mueller-Hanson and colleagues' (2005) conclusion that openness to experience is resistant to change via training. However, we did not include openness to experience in Figure 5.1, as it was not one of the primary constructs in our review.

Figure 5.1
Degree of Malleability of ALRM Constructs

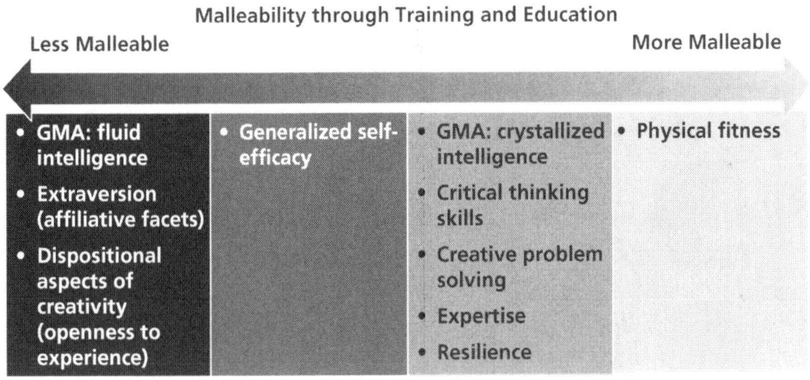

Constructs that may be malleable through work experiences or organizational practices

- Conscientiousness
- Extraversion (social dominance facets)
- Affective commitment

Insufficient research evidence regarding malleability

- Dispositional aspects of critical thinking
- Metacognition
- Emotional intelligence
- Ethical decisionmaking
- Initiative
- Motivation to lead

SOURCE: Adapted from Mueller-Hanson et al., 2005.
RAND *RR1583-5.1*

skills can be developed through training and education. Likewise, evidence indicates that training interventions can contribute to development of resilience.

Mueller-Hanson et al. (2005) concluded that domain-specific knowledge is readily modifiable with training. Our review of expertise concurs with this finding, although change occurs slowly and becoming an expert can take many years to achieve. We conclude that physical fitness can be developed through training, as well. There is also evidence that training can improve CT skills, particularly domain-specific CT.

Mueller-Hanson and her colleagues concluded that metacognitive skills and GSE are amenable to change (to varied degrees) but that considerable effort is needed to bring about such change. We concur with this conclusion about GSE. However, there is insufficient research regarding the malleability of metacognitive skills in work contexts. There also is limited or insufficient research or conflicting findings about the malleability of EI, ethical decisionmaking, initiative, and motivation to lead.

The degree to which ALRM attributes are modifiable through training and education raises questions about the return on investment (ROI) of programs designed to develop these attributes. In light of the effort needed to bring about changes in some constructs, and the lack of evidence regarding the degree of malleability of others, a critical question for the Army is to determine whether ROI is greater for selection and placement strategies compared to training and development interventions.

Utility analysis (UA) is an approach that has been used to estimate the economic value of personnel practices (e.g., Cascio, 1989; Schmidt, Hunter, and Pearlman, 1982). UA has been used primarily in the area of employee selection, and to a lesser extent for other personnel programs, including training and development (see Arthur et al., 2003; Cascio, 1989). Whereas calculating the costs of training may be relatively straightforward, estimating the benefits, in terms of dollar value, is much more challenging; such analyses are conducted infrequently compared to evaluating other types of training outcomes in organizations (e.g., Aragón-Sánchez, Barba-Aragón, and Sanz-Valle, 2003; Arthur et al., 2003). Methods of UA that measure benefits in terms of the gain associated with improved job performance could be used to determine the value of efforts to develop ALRM attributes through training.

What Types of Measures Should Be Used?

For many of the constructs we have discussed, there are different approaches to measurement, such as tests, surveys, work sample tests, and interviews. Key considerations when selecting the type of measure to use include reliability, validity, scalability, response burden, and cost. Reliability and validity are essential considerations when selecting measures. Other factors, the ability to collect data from large numbers of respondents, the amount of burden placed on the participants to respond, and the direct and indirect costs associated with an instrument, represent more practical considerations. Where possible, we recommend use of self-report measures, including tests (e.g., of knowledge or skills) or surveys (e.g., of attitudes or dispositions) with established reliability and validity. Tests and surveys can be used to measure a range of constructs. Written tests and surveys administered using paper and pencil or by computer that use forced-choice (i.e., multiple-choice) questions are also advantageous in that they provide objective measures (i.e., quantitative data, and in the case of tests, right or wrong answers) and can be administered and scored using automated methods.[2] Thus, these methods of testing are highly scalable.

Another advantage of using instruments with forced-choice responses is the potential application of computer-adaptive testing (CAT) methods. CAT is a statistical procedure that tailors the test or survey questions based on the test taker's responses to the items. For example, a test taker who correctly answers an initial question that is moderately difficult would then be presented with a more difficult item, whereas a test taker who answers the initial question incorrectly would be presented with an easier item. The process works in the same way for surveys, using the extent to which respondents' answers are more or less extreme with respect to the attitude or dispositional trait being measured. This process is iterative and proceeds until a reliable estimate of construct is obtained. By generating tests or surveys with fewer items, CAT lowers response burden. CAT also enhances test security because each respondent gets a different set of items. Forced-choice measures can be challenging and costly to construct (particularly when using CAT), but once developed, they can be administered and scored efficiently on a large-scale basis.

A downside of many forced-choice measures is that it may be easy for respondents to fake, thereby compromising validity. The intent of such

---

[2] Whereas some studies use surveys to measure respondents' perceptions of their knowledge or skills, it is preferable to use tests that have right answers because self-reported knowledge and skills are subject to faking good. Perceptions of knowledge and skills are appropriate when measuring self-efficacy, however, which by definition reflects individuals' attitudes about their competence.

measures and which responses are more desirable may be especially apparent in instruments that use single-stimulus items, such as when respondents report how often they engage in particular behaviors or the degree to which adjectives or statements describe them. Some strategies have been used to attempt to detect faking good (such as including "lie scales" in surveys or analyzing responses to identify inconsistent patterns), or to correct for socially desirable responses post hoc (e.g., Ferrando and Anguiano-Carrasco, 2013; Griffith and McDaniel, 2006; Goffin and Christiansen, 2003), but there is disagreement about the effectiveness of these alternatives. Forced-choice measures using paired-comparisons or SJTs can diminish faking good but are more labor intensive to develop.

In contrast, it is reasonable to expect that "faking good" or providing socially desirable responses is less problematic when using tests or surveys using constructed-response (open-ended) questions. In addition, some scholars argue that constructed-response tests produce better assessments of constructs such as higher-order cognitive processes and better reflect tasks in actual job settings (see Zaccaro et al., 2000, for a review). However, constructed-response tests are much less scalable. While constructed-response tests can be administered to large groups of people simultaneously, the tests typically take longer to administer and, therefore, impose greater response burden. They are also much more labor-intensive and costly to score in that they typically require evaluation by SMEs. SMEs often need to be trained to ensure they are consistent in their evaluations. Even with training, rating constructed responses involves subjective judgment and, therefore, can be influenced by cognitive biases and rater errors.[3]

[3] Some organizations have developed automated (electronic) approaches to score open-ended questions. This approach can be relatively straightforward and computationally simple for evaluating some skills, such as the clarity of written communication (e.g., the Flesch-Kincaid readability tests; Flesch, 1948). In fact, the Flesch-Kincaid readability formula has existed for decades; it is the DOD military standard for assessing the reading difficulty or grade level of documents, and it is a feature in off-the-shelf word processing software. Some testing companies have developed more advanced algorithms to evaluate the mechanics, organization, and content of participant's responses to standardized writing prompts, but these approaches may miss some of the contextual or subtler aspects of responses that open-ended questions are intended to elicit.

In some cases, observers rate individuals on particular attributes. This approach may reduce some of the issues arising with the use of self-reports, but it is also subject to a number of constraints and shortcomings. Observers must have sufficient knowledge to provide accurate ratings, including knowledge of the relevant topic areas and knowledge of the person being evaluated (i.e., raters must have sufficient opportunities to observe the person being rated). Observers must also be motivated to provide accurate ratings; in some organizations, raters are reluctant to be forthright, particularly with respect to providing negative feedback. In addition, "other" ratings are subject to unintentional cognitive biases or rater errors, such as halo error.

Our review also discussed the use of work sample tests and interviews to measure some constructs. Work sample tests are particularly good for assessing less tangible skills or knowledge and skills not amenable to measurement using paper-and-pencil tests. Work sample tests also have high face validity, i.e., test takers and other stakeholders view them as relevant and fair. However, work sample tests typically have low scalability; they are costly to develop, often require one-on-one administration, and, like constructed-response tests, may require human judges who are trained to provide reliable ratings.

Finally, researchers have used interviews to assess some of ALRM-relevant constructs, such as expertise and initiative. Interviews have many of the same disadvantages as work sample tests, in that they are conducted on an individual basis and, therefore, are time consuming to administer. Interviews also involve subjective judgment, which is prone to biases. Using a structured approach can alleviate some of these issues. Ultimately, if available, we recommend using reliable and valid self-report instruments rather than interviews to assess constructs related to the ALRM.

What Constructs Should Be Assessed?

There are numerous constructs that might be relevant in studies of leader attributes and competencies. Clearly, the topic of study should guide the choice of measures. For example, if studying effects of training to improve CT, relevant measures are likely to include assessments of CT skills and dispositions. In addition, the measures should "match" or correspond to the nature of the intervention in question. For example, if the intervention addresses general CT skills, then one of the domain-general measures identified in this report would be appropriate. If the intervention is focused on specific CT skills, e.g., on cognitive biases and heuristics, then a test of those concepts would be used. In addition, measuring potential correlates of the topic in question (for CT skills, these might include GMA and metacognition) can help determine the strength of the intervention; i.e., the degree to which the outcome can be explained by the intervention or by other factors that are related to the outcome. We advocate a theory-driven approach to guide construct selection when assessing the effectiveness of training interventions.

A different example pertains to the Big Five factors. As described in earlier chapters, the Big Five consist of narrower facets, and the selection of facets to measure should correspond to the topic of study. For example, as noted in Chapter Four, the social dominance aspect of extraversion, but not the affiliative aspect, is positively associated with leadership (Do and Minbashian, 2014) and there is evidence of change in social dominance across the lifespan (Roberts, Walton, and Viechtbauer, 2006). In their meta-analysis of the association of conscientiousness facets and job performance, Dudley, Orvis, Lebiecki, and Cortina (2006) found that facets of conscientiousness did not explain job performance beyond global measures of conscientiousness, but facets did contribute to explaining contextual performance, such as extra-role behaviors and job dedication.

When and How Should Measures Be Used?

Design Studies to Rule out Threats to Validity

When studying the extent to which training and education interventions lead to improvement in key constructs, the study design, in part, determines the kinds of conclusions that one can draw. Different combinations of the pretest and posttest measures and the intervention allow one to rule out threats to internal validity of the study, i.e., factors that prevent the researcher from drawing conclusions about the effects of the intervention.[4] A research design that can rule out many of these threats is the pretest posttest control group design, which consists of two conditions, as shown in Figure 5.2 (Campbell and Stanley, 1963). For example, if studying the effects of a CT training intervention, participants in Group 1 complete the CT skills test along with measures of relevant covariates prior to training (pretest measures, or O_1), participate in training (X), and complete the CT skills tests after training (O_2). Participants in Group 2 complete the same measures at the same time as Group 1 but do not participate in the intervention. This approach allows one to determine whether the intervention has the intended effect and rules out most threats to internal validity. Additional groups can rule out other threats to internal validity. Including similar conditions to Groups 1 and 2, without the pretest (i.e., X-O_2 and O_2 only), allows one to determine the interaction of testing and the intervention. Collecting subsequent measures over time (e.g., O_3, O_4) can also be included to assess retention of knowledge and skills.

Random assignment of participants to these groups safeguards against selection effects so that participants in both groups do not vary systematically in important characteristics that might affect performance on the tests or responses to the intervention. That is, random assignment helps ensure that changes in the outcome of interest occur because of the intervention rather than because of characteristics of the participants in each group.

In many organizational settings, however, random assignment and/or using ideal experimental conditions are not feasible. For example, random assignment might not be possible because it means withholding an intervention from personnel. Administering a pretest might not be practical if training or experience is needed before personnel can attempt the task (e.g., if the task is highly complex or poses safety concerns). Thus, quasi-experimental methods are frequently implemented, in which a

---

[4] As described by Campbell and Stanley, common threats to internal validity include history (events occurring between O_1 and O_2); maturation (processes corresponding to the passage of time that affect participants, such as aging or physiological responses; e.g., fatigue); testing (the effects of taking the first test on responses to the second test); instrumentation (changes in the measure or observers that influence measurements); and statistical regression (which occurs when selection to groups is based on extreme scores).

Figure 5.2
Pretest Posttest Control Group Design

Group	PreTest measure (O_1)	Intervention (X)	PreTest Measure (O_2)
1	O_1	X	O_2
2	O_1		O_2

NOTE: O = observation, X = intervention.
RAND RR1583-5.2

subset of the conditions is used (e.g., O_1-X-O_2 and X-O_2) and/or participants are not randomly assigned to conditions. When random assignment is not possible, it is especially important to measure and control for characteristics of participants that might affect responses to the intervention.

Administer or Collect Measures of Some Constructs for Officers on a Routine Basis

For the Army as a whole, we recommend collecting baseline data from officers that can be used for job placement as well as for ongoing study efforts. Whereas Army enlisted personnel complete tests of GMA (i.e., the ASVAB) and dispositional constructs (i.e., Big Five factors) during recruitment, to our knowledge the Army does not systematically administer or collect such measures for officers. The Army might have records of GMA measures for officers as reflected by college grade-point average and college admissions test scores, but the Army does not systematically use these scores for job placement or routinely use these data in ongoing studies. In light of the relevance of GMA and the Big Five to many of the ALRM attributes and performance, collecting these measures prior to or upon commissioning could prove useful for job placement and for use in ongoing Army research (e.g., to understand the effects of training and a range of other interventions or topics of interest). Given that the Army selects senior officers from existing officer ranks, baseline measures of these constructs and other ALRM attributes, coupled with routine reassessments over time (e.g., during key leader education courses), can help the Army understand how long-term interventions and experiences influence key Army intellectual, presence, and character attributes, including attributes that are malleable but develop gradually over time. Assessing changes over time is especially important in that some attributes might predict leader outcomes when measured later in one's career but not at entry (e.g., Chan and Drasgow, 2001). Thus, routine assessment and analysis could address questions regarding the ROI or utility of educational efforts and other developmental experiences for Army leaders.

Limitations and Topics for Future Research

Additional Constructs for Review

While we have attempted to be comprehensive in this review, we did not address all relevant constructs associated with ALRM attributes or leader effectiveness. First, we excluded constructs for which there is limited research or a lack of established measures. Second, we did not review constructs associated with leader effectiveness that do not reflect attributes specified in the ALRM. Third, we had limited discussion of situational variables that moderate or affect the expression of leader attributes. We review some of these constructs here.

Three variables that are related to intellect attributes in the ALRM and for which there is relatively limited research are *cognitive flexibility, adaptive expertise*, and *frame-switching capabilities*, which are relevant to mental agility, and *social intelligence*, which is relevant to interpersonal tact.

Cognitive flexibility is defined as "a person's (a) awareness that in any given situation there are options and alternatives available, (b) willingness to be flexible and adapt to the situation, and (c) self-efficacy in being flexible" (Martin and Rubin, 1995, p. 623). This definition appears highly related to constructs associated with the ARLM attribute of mental agility, such as openness to experience and divergent thinking. Martin and his colleagues developed and tested a 12-item scale of cognitive flexibility (Martin and Anderson, 1998; Martin and Rubin, 1995),[5] but this scale has been used sparingly in workplace research

[5] Example items include "I can find workable solutions to seemingly unsolvable problems" and "I am willing to listen and consider alternatives for handling a problem."

(see Zaccaro et al., 2009, for an exception). Thus, more evidence is needed regarding the distinctiveness of cognitive flexibility and related constructs.

Adaptive expertise refers to individuals' ability to apply their expert knowledge to invent new procedures and solve novel problems (Holyoak, 1991). Scholars suggest by having a deep conceptual understanding of a particular domain (i.e., more abstract representations of domain knowledge), experts can apply this knowledge to new situations that vary in superficial characteristics (Kimball and Holyoak, 2000; Smith, Ford, and Kozlowski, 1997). Frame-switching, which is the capacity to change one's perspective or frame of reference when solving problems, is considered a fundamental element of adaptive expertise (see Nelson, Zaccaro, and Herman, 2010, for a review). In addition, evidence shows that frame-switching and adaptive expertise can be developed through training as well as developmental experiences and contributes to adaptive performance (see Nelson, Zaccaro, and Herman, 2010; Smith, Ford, and Kozlowski, 1997).[6]

Social intelligence is a construct with relevance to the attribute of interpersonal tact. Social intelligence refers to skills related to intrapersonal (ability to understand one's own feelings) and interpersonal (ability to understand other people's moods, mental states, etc.) activities and act appropriately in these various interactions (e.g., Brislin, Worthley, and Macnab, 2006; Salovey and Mayer, 1990). Although this construct dates back to the first part of the twentieth century (see Landy, 2006), it has been largely overlooked in favor of EI (see Kobe, Reiter-Palmon,

---

[6] Interesting, many researchers have discussed a trade-off between expertise and cognitive flexibility; as one gains expertise, they can become less able to consider alternative approaches to problem solving, have trouble adapting to novel situations, and have more difficulty generating radical or groundbreaking ideas (see Dane, 2010, for a review). Dane (2010) refers to this lack of flexibility as *cognitive entrenchment* and proposes that it can be mitigated when operating in dynamic environments (which arguably is the case for Army leaders) and by paying attention to situations outside of one's primary domain of expertise. Smith, Ford, and Kozlowski (1997) argue that adaptive expertise requires development of not only deep knowledge structures, which can be developed through practice, but through activation of metacognitive skills. They propose training strategies to foster adaptive expertise, including use of advance organizers, analogies, discovery learning, error-based training, metacognitive instruction, learner control, and mastery-oriented learning.

and Rickers, 2001; Zaccaro, Gilbert, Thor, and Mumford, 1991, for some exceptions). Only recently has social intelligence received a resurgence of scholarly attention (e.g., Crowne, 2009; Goleman and Boyatzis, 2008; Riggio and Reichard, 2008; Weis and Süβ, 2007). One noteworthy challenge confronting research on social intelligence is clarification of its relationship to related variables—specifically EI. Some researchers consider EI to be a subset of social intelligence (e.g., Salovey and Mayer, 1990), whereas others propose the two are the same construct (e.g., Bar-On, Tranel, Denburg, and Bechara, 2003). Those in the "distinct" camp argue that EI is limited to emotional information, whereas social intelligence goes beyond emotions to include social information more broadly. For example, individuals may be high on social intelligence because they can function effectively in various social scenarios such as business meetings or working lunches (e.g., by processing social information, maintaining social awareness and demonstrating appropriate social skills such as introducing oneself and interacting properly); however, they may be low on EI because they may be ill-equipped to manage emotional situations such as responding to a person who is yelling or crying (e.g., Crowne, 2009). In short, individuals with high EI are also expected to be high in social intelligence, but the reverse is not necessarily true, which is why this camp suggests that EI and social intelligence are distinct. Conceptual clarification between social intelligence and EI would also contribute to an understanding of how social intelligence is related to other constructs, such as perspective taking, which is the attempt to understand the thoughts, motives, and feelings of another person (Parker and Axtell, 2001) and which has been subject to some workplace research (e.g., Grant and Berry, 2011; Hoever, van Knippenberg, van Ginkel, and Barkema, 2012).

Constructs associated with leadership effectiveness but not identified explicitly in the ALRM include *adaptability* and *systems thinking*. In light of evidence for the association of these constructs with leader performance, the Army should consider inclusion of these constructs in future iterations of the ALRM.

Adaptability is a construct that has received increasing attention in the Army. Adaptive leadership is a central concept in the U.S. Army's human dimension strategy (U.S. Department of the Army, 2015) and is emphasized in the ALRM. Army FM 6-22 (Headquarters, Department of the Army, 2015) defines adaptability as "an effective change in behavior in response to an altered or unexpected situation" (p. 5-7). Studies have found evidence for an association of adaptability and leader performance (e.g., Hannah et al., 2013; Yukl and Mahsud, 2010; Zaccaro, Foti, and Kenny, 1991) and have shown that aspects of adaptability can be developed in Army leaders through training and education (Straus et al., 2014). Defining, measuring, and altering adaptability, however, is not straightforward. Adaptability is a multidimensional construct consisting of cognitive and social skills and dispositions. The most influential work in this area to date is from Pulakos, Arad, Donovan, and Plamondon (2000), who developed and tested a taxonomy consisting of eight factors: solving problems creatively; learning tasks, technologies, and procedures; dealing with unpredictable or changing working situations; handling emergencies or crisis situations; handling work stress; interpersonal adaptability; cultural adaptability, and physical adaptability. As described by Baard, Rench, and Kozlowski (2013), adaptability has been defined in different ways; e.g., as an individual attribute, as performance, as changes in performance, and as a process. These approaches have different implications regarding the malleability of adaptability and, if malleable, appropriate methods of training and education. There are also many measures of adaptability, with limited evidence of construct and criterion-related validity (see Baard, Rench, and Kozlowski, 2013).

Systems thinking (also referred to as cognitive complexity and strategic thinking) involves highly conceptual skills to adopt a big-picture perspective to understand complexity, deal with uncertainty, and bring about change (e.g., Hooijberg, Hunt, and Dodge, 1997; Katz and Khan, 1978; Mumford, Campion, Morgeson, 2007; Zaccaro, 2001). This construct involves the capacity to create a mental map defining and organizing important elements, interactions, and interrelationships among multiple organizational units, subsystems, and components, as well as the ability to forecast potential events and their outcomes across increasingly longer time horizons (e.g., Jacobs and Jaques, 1987; Zaccaro, 2001). This skill appears particularly important at the most senior levels of leadership (Hooijberg, Hunt, and Dodge,

1997; Mumford, Campion, and Morgeson, 2007; Zaccaro, 2001). The complexity of the Army's organizational structure and operations suggests the need for systems thinking in Army leaders.

Situational characteristics comprise other variables to consider in future research on fostering ALRM attributes and competencies. Theories of leadership have long considered influences of situational factors on leader effectiveness (e.g., see Stogdill, 1950). Throughout this report, we have mentioned moderating effects of situational variables, such as task characteristics, on the association of leader attributes and performance, but we have not systematically reviewed the role of situational factors. We expect that organizational culture is another important situational factor to consider. Organizational culture, as defined by Schein (1990), consists of shared assumptions that organizational members develop to cope with problems of external adaptation and internal integration, consider valid, and teach to new members as ways to think about and respond to those problems. Organizational culture and the related concept of organizational climate influence constructs relevant to the ALRM, such as innovation (Hammond et al., 2011) and ethical behavior (O'Fallon and Butterfield, 2005). Moreover, leaders both create organizational culture and are defined and created by it (Schein, 2004); a recent review by Meredith et al. (2017) describes the role of leaders at all levels in shaping Army culture and climate. With respect to the ALRM, it is important to understand how task characteristics, organizational culture, and other situational factors affect development and expression of leader attributes.

Additional Directions for Future Research

Leadership is a complex construct, and there are many additional topics to address in future research.

First, as we have discussed in this report, some ALRM attributes, particularly warrior ethos and service ethos, and military and professional bearing, do not correspond directly to established constructs and extant measures. Greater clarity about these attributes could facilitate leader development and measurement efforts with respect to presence and character characteristics, respectively. In addition, as shown in Tables 1.1 through 1.3, several established constructs associated with leadership correspond to different attributes within and/or across intellect, presence, and character categories. A better understanding of associations among ALRM attributes—for example, distinguishing distal and proximal predictors (Allen et al., 2014; Chan and Drasgow, 2001; Van Iddekinge, Ferris, and Heffner, 2009; Zaccaro, 2007) and identifying how patterns or constellations of attributes predict leadership (Foti and Hauenstein, 2007; Zaccaro, Kemp, and Bader, 2004)—could foster knowledge to support leader selection and development efforts.[7]

Second, we have not identified all possible measures of the constructs we reviewed. There may be other instruments suitable for the evaluation of ALRM attributes. A related topic is that the reliability and validity of measures may not generalize to specific target populations and, therefore, may need to be established within the context of the Army.

Third, as mentioned throughout this report, more research is needed on a number of attributes with respect to associations with leader performance, malleability, and/or development or validation of measures. In addition, our discussion of the Big Five characteristics associated with ALRM attributes suggests the need for finer-grained investigations. That is, studies vary in the extent to which they measure the Big Five at the attribute or facet level. These distinctions are important in that some facets might be more malleable through training than others (e.g., Roberts, Walton, and Viechtbauer, 2006), vary in their association with aspects of leader performance (e.g., Do and Minbashian, 2014; Judge et al., 2002), or exert opposing forces on performance (Judge and Zapata, 2015).

Finally, our review focused on development of key attributes in leaders, but we did not address in detail the role of leaders in developing these attributes in others. "Develops others" is one of the compe-

[7] Proximal attributes are those that predict leader outcomes directly and often interact with characteristics of the situation. Distal attributes are those that predict leader outcomes less directly, often by influencing proximal variables. Zaccaro, Kemp, and Bader's (2004) model of leader attributes conceptualizes distal attributes as more trait-like, such as GMA and personality traits, and proximal attributes as more state-like, such as social skills, problem-solving skills, and expertise.

tencies in the ALRM, and research shows that leader behavior is an important factor in fostering attributes—such as creativity and innovation (Hammond et al., 2011; Shin and Zhou, 2007; Tierney and Farmer, 2011; Zhang and Zhou, 2014), affective commitment (Avolio, Zhu, Koh, and Bhatia, 2004; Meyer et al., 2002), and hardiness (Bartone, 2006)—in others. Thus, we suggest that leader training and education address which attributes are more or less malleable, and for attributes that can be changed, provide strategies for developing these attributes in others. In addition, whereas this report focuses on ALRM attributes, a comprehensive review of leader competencies could prove fruitful. Taken together, these efforts can enhance the Army's understanding of the factors that contribute to effective leadership and can guide leader development and selection practices.

Abbreviations

ACQ	Affective Commitment Questionnaire
ADMC	Adult Decision-Making Competence
ADRP	Army Doctrine Reference Publication
AFQT	Armed Forces Qualification Test
ALRM	Army Leader Requirements Model
AOT	Actively Open-Minded Thinking
APFT	Army Physical Fitness Test
ASVAB	Armed Services Vocational Aptitude Battery
CAT	computer-adaptive testing
CPS	Creative Personality Scale
CT	critical thinking
DIT	Defining Issues Test
DOI	Decision Outcomes Inventory
DRS	Dispositional Resilience Scale
ECI	Emotional Competence Inventory
EI	emotional intelligence
ELS	Ethical Leadership Scale
EQ-I	Emotional Quotient Inventory
GMA	General Mental Ability
GPSE	General Perceived Self-Efficacy
GRE	Graduate Record Examination
GSE	general self-efficacy
HPI	Hogan Personality Inventory
IPIP	International Personality Item Pool

KSAOs	Knowledge, Skills, Abilities, and Other Characteristics
LOT	Life Orientation Test
MAI	Metacognitive Awareness Inventory
MAT	Miller Analogies Test
MEPS	Military Entrance Processing Stations
MMFT	Mindfulness-Based Mind Fitness Training
MSCEIT	Mayer-Salovey-Caruso Emotional Intelligence Test
MTL	motivation to lead
NEO PI-R	Neuroticism-Extraversion-Openness Personality Inventory-Revised
NGSE	New Generalized Self-Efficacy
OCQ	Organizational Commitment Questionnaire
OPAT	Occupational Physical Assessment Test
PVS	Personal Views Survey
ROI	return on investment
SJT	situational judgment tests
SME	subject matter expert
TAPAS	Tailored Adaptive Personality Assessment System
TKML	Tacit Knowledge for Military Leaders
UA	utility analysis
WLEIS	Wong and Law Emotional Intelligence Scale

References

Abrami, P. C., R. M. Bernard, E. Borokhovski, D. I. Waddington, C. A. Wade, and T. Persson, "Strategies for Teaching Students to Think Critically: A Meta-Analysis," *Review of Educational Research*, Vol. 85, No. 2, 2015, pp. 275–314.

Abrami, P. C., R. M. Bernard, E. Borokhovski, A. Wade, M. A. Surkes, R. Tamim, and D. Zhang, "Instructional Interventions Affecting Critical Thinking Skills and Dispositions: A Stage 1 Meta-Analysis," *Review of Educational Research*, Vol. 78, No. 4, 2008, pp. 1102–1134.

Adler, A. B., C. A. Castro, and D. McGurk, "Time-Driven Battlemind Psychological Debriefing: A Group-Level Early Intervention in Combat," *Military Medicine*, Vol. 174, 2009, pp. 22–28.

Allen, M. J., and W. M. Yen, *Introduction to Measurement Theory*, Belmont, Calif.: Wadsworth, 1979.

Allen, M. T., B. H. Bynum, J. T. Oliver, T. L. Russell, M. C. Young, and N. E. Babin, "Predicting Leadership Performance and Potential in the U.S. Army Officer Candidate School (OCS)," *Military Psychology*, Vol. 26, No. 4, 2014, pp. 310–326.

Allen, N. J., and J. P. Meyer, "The Measurement and Antecedent of Affective, Continuance, and Normative Commitment to the Organization," *Journal of Occupational Psychology*, Vol. 63, 1990, pp. 1–18.

Amit, K., A. Lisak, M. Popper, and R. Gal, "Motivation to Lead: Research on the Motives for Undertaking Leadership Roles in the Israel Defense Forces (IDF)," *Military Psychology*, Vol. 19, No. 3, 2007, pp. 137–160.

Anderson, J. R., *The Architecture of Cognition*, Cambridge, Mass.: Harvard University Press, 1983.

Antonakis, J., J. Hedlund, J. E. Pretz, and R. J. Sternberg, "Exploring the Nature and Acquisition of Tacit Knowledge for Military Leadership," Research Note 2002-04, Alexandria, Va.: U.S. Army Research Institute for the Behavioral and Social Sciences, 2002.

Aragón-Sánchez, A., I. Barba-Aragón, and R. Sanz-Valle, "Effects of Training on Business Results," *International Journal of Human Resource Management*, Vol. 14, No. 6, September 2003, pp. 956–980.

Arthur, Jr., W., W. Bennett, Jr., P. S. Edens, and S. T. Bell, "Effectiveness of Training in Organizations: A Meta-Analysis of Design and Evaluation Features," *Journal of Applied Psychology*, Vol. 88, No. 2, 2003, pp. 234–245.

Atwater, L. E., S. D. Dionne, B. Avolio, J. F. Camobreco, and A. W. Lau, "A Longitudinal Study of the Leadership Development Process: Individual Differences Predicting Leader Effectiveness," *Human Relations*, Vol. 52, No. 12, 1999, pp. 1543–1562.

Atwater, L. E., S. D. Dionne, J. F. Camobreco, B. J. Avolio, and A. Lau, "Individual Attributes and Leadership Style: Predicting the Use of Punishment and Its Effects," *Journal of Organizational Behavior*, Vol. 19, 1998, pp. 559–576.

Atwater, L. E., and F. J. Yammarino, "Personal Attributes as Predictors of Superiors' and Subordinates' Perceptions of Military Academy Leadership," *Human Relations*, Vol. 46, 1993, pp. 645–668.

Au, J., E. Sheehan, N. Tsai, G. J. Duncan, M. Buschkuehl, and S. M. Jaeggi, "Improving Fluid Intelligence with Training on Working Memory: A Meta-Analysis," *Psychonomic Bulletin & Review*, Vol. 22, 2014, pp. 366–377.

Aude, S. N., J. Bryson, H. Keller-Glaze, K. Nicely, and C. L. Vowels, *Preparing Brigade Combat Team Soldiers for Mission Readiness Through Research on Intangible Psychological Constructs and Their Applications: Phase I*, Arlington, Va.: U.S. Army Research Institute for the Behavioral and Social Sciences, Technical Report 1336, 2014.

Avolio, B. J., W. Zhu, W. Koh, and P. Bhatia, "Transformational Leadership and Organizational Commitment: Mediating Role of Psychological Empowerment and Moderating Role of Structural Distance," *Journal of Organizational Behavior*, Vol. 25, No. 8, 2004, pp. 951–968.

Baard, S. K., T. A. Rench, and S. W. J. Kozlowski, "Performance Adaptation: A Theoretical Integration and Review," *Journal of Management*, Vol. 40, No. 1, 2013, pp. 48–99.

Bandura, A., "Self-Efficacy: Toward a Unifying Theory of Behavioral Change," *Psychological Review*, Vol. 84, No. 2, 1977, pp. 191–215.

———, "Self-Efficacy Mechanism in Human Agency," *American Psychologist*, Vol. 37, No. 2, 1982, pp. 122–147.

———, *Self-Efficacy: The Exercise of Control*, New York: W. H. Freeman and Company, 1997.

———, "Social Cognitive Theory of Personality," in L. Pervin and O. John, eds., *Handbook of Personality: Theory and Research*, 1999, pp. 154–196.

Bandura, A., N. E. Adams, A. B. Hardy, and G. N. Howells, "Tests of the Generality of Self-Efficacy Theory," *Cognitive Therapy and Research*, Vol. 4, 1980, pp. 39–66.

Baran, B. E., and C. W. Scott, "Organizing Ambiguity: A Grounded Theory of Leadership and Sensemaking Within Dangerous Contexts," *Military Psychology*, Vol. 22, 2010, pp. S42–S69.

Bar-On, R., *BarOn Emotional Quotient Inventory: Technical Manual*, Toronto, Ont.: Multi-Health Systems, 1997.

———, "The Bar-On Model of Emotional-Social Intelligence (ESI)," *Psicothema*, Vol. 18, suppl., 2006, pp. 13–25.

Bar-On, R., D. Tranel, N. L. Denburg, and A. Bechara, "Exploring the Neurological Substrate of Emotional and Social Intelligence," *Brain*, Vol. 126, No. 8, 2003, pp. 1790–1800.

Barrick, M. R., and M. K. Mount, "The Big Five Personality Dimensions and Job Performance: A Meta-Analysis," *Personnel Psychology*, Vol. 44, 1991, pp. 1–26.

Bartone P. T., "A Short Hardiness Scale," paper presented at the Annual Convention of the American Psychological Society, New York, July 1995.

———, "Resilience Under Military Operational Stress: Can Leaders Influence Hardiness?" *Military Psychology*, Vol. 18, suppl., 2006, S131–S148.

———, "Test-Retest Reliability of the Dispositional Resilience Scale-15, a Brief Hardiness Scale," *Psychological Reports*, Vol. 101, 2007, pp. 943–944.

Bartone, P. T., J. Eid, B. H. Johnsen, J. C. Laberg, and S. A. Snook, "Big Five Personality Factors, Hardiness, and Social Judgment as Predictors of Leader Performance," *Leadership & Organization Development Journal*, Vol. 30, 2009, pp. 498–521.

Bartone, P. T., D. R. Kelly, and M. D. Matthews, "Psychological Hardiness Predicts Adaptability in Military Leaders: A Prospective Study," *International Journal of Selection and Assessment*, Vol. 21, No. 2, 2013, pp. 200–210.

Bartone, P. T., R. R. Roland, J. J. Picano, and T. J. Williams, "Psychological Hardiness Predicts Success in U.S. Army Special Forces Candidates," *International Journal of Selection and Assessment*, Vol. 16, 2008, pp. 78–81.

Bartone, P. T., S. A. Snook, and T. R. Tremble, "Cognitive and Personality Predictors of Leader Performance in West Point Cadets," *Military Psychology*, Vol. 14, No. 4, 2002, pp. 321–338.

Bass, B. M., *Leadership and Performance Beyond Expectations*, New York: Free Press, 1985.

———, *The Bass Handbook of Leadership: Theory, Research and Managerial Applications*, 4th ed., New York: Free Press, 2008.

Bassyiouny, M., *Modification and Evaluation of a Personal Initiative Training for Job Seekers*, thesis, University of Giessen, 2007.

Bateman, T. S., and J. M. Crant, "The Proactive Component of Organizational Behavior: A Measure and Correlates," *Journal of Organizational Behavior*, Vol. 14, 1993, pp. 103–118.

Batey, M., *A Psychometric Investigation of Everyday Creativity*, dissertation, University of London, 2007.

Bledow, R., and M. Frese, "A Situational Judgment Test of Personal Initiative and Its Relationship to Performance," *Personnel Psychology*, Vol. 62, 2009, pp. 229–258.

Bonanno, G. A., "Loss, Trauma, and Human Resilience: Have We Underestimated the Human Capacity to Thrive after Extremely Aversive Events?" *American Psychologist*, Vol. 59, No. 1, 2004, pp. 20–28.

Boyatzis, R. E., and A. Saatcioglu, "A 20-Year View of Trying to Develop Emotional, Social and Cognitive Intelligence Competencies in Graduate Management Education," *Journal of Management Development*, Vol. 27, 2008, pp. 92–108.

Boyatzis, R. E., and F. Sala, "The Emotional Competence Inventory (ECI)," in G. Geher, ed., *Measuring Emotional Intelligence: Common Ground and Controversy*, Hauppauge, N.Y.: Nova Science Publishers, 2004, pp. 147–180.

Brislin, R., T. Worthley, and B. Macnab, "Cultural Intelligence: Understanding Behaviors that Serve People's Goals," *Group & Organization Management*, Vol. 31, No. 1, 2006, pp. 40–55.

Brown, J. D., "Exercise as a Buffer of Life Stress: A Prospective Study of Adolescent Health," *Health Psychology*, Vol. 7, No. 4, 1988, pp. 341–353.

———, "Staying Fit and Staying Well: Physical Fitness as a Moderator of Life Stress," *Journal of Personality and Social Psychology*, Vol. 60, No. 4, May 1991, pp. 555–561.

Brown, J. I., V. V. Fishco, and G. Hanna, *The Nelson-Denny Reading Test*, Itasca, Ill.: The Riverside Publishing Company, 1993.

Brown, M. E., and L. K. Treviño, "Ethical Leadership: A Review and Future Directions," *The Leadership Quarterly*, Vol. 17, No. 6, 2006, pp. 595–616.

Brown, M. E., L. K. Treviño, and D. A. Harrison, "Ethical Leadership: A Social Learning Perspective for Construct Development and Testing," *Organizational Behavior and Human Decision Processes*, Vol. 97, No. 2, 2005, pp. 117–134.

Bruine de Bruin, W., A. M. Parker, and B. Fischhoff, "Individual Differences in Adult Decision-Making Competence," *Journal of Personality and Social Psychology*, Vol. 92, No. 5, 2007, pp. 938–956.

Buschkuehl, M., and S. M. Jaeggi, "Improving Intelligence: A Literature Review," *Swiss Medical Weekly*, Vol. 140, No. 19–20, 2010, pp. 266–272.

Butler, H. A., C. P. Dwyer, M. J. Hogan, A. Franco, S. F. Rivas, C. Saiz, and L. S. Almeida, "The Halpern Critical Thinking Assessment and Real-World Outcomes: Cross-National Applications," *Thinking Skills and Creativity*, Vol. 7, No. 2, 2012, pp. 112–121.

Cacioppo, J. T., R. E. Petty, J. A. Feinstein, and W. B. B. Jarvis, "Dispositional Differences in Cognitive Motivation: The Life and Times of Individuals Varying in Need for Cognition," *Psychological Bulletin*, Vol. 119, No. 2, 1996, pp. 197–253.

Callinan, M., and I. T. Robertson, "Work Sample Testing," *International Journal of Selection and Assessment*, Vol. 8, No. 4, 2000, pp. 248–260.

Campbell, D. T., and J. C. Stanley, *Experimental and Quasi-Experimental Designs for Research*, Boston, Mass.: Houghton-Mifflin, 1963.

Carr, W., D. Bradley, A. D. Ogle, S. E. Eonta, B. L. Pyle, and P. Santiago, "Resilience Training in a Population of Deployed Personnel," *Military Psychology*, Vol. 25, No. 2, March 2013, pp. 148–155.

Carroll, J. B., *Human Cognitive Abilities: A Survey of Factor-Analytic Studies*, New York: Cambridge University Press, 1993.

Carver, C. S., "Life Orientation Test-Revised (LOT-R)," *Measurement Instrument Database for the Social Science*, 2013. As of December 27, 2016: http://www.midss.org/sites/default/files/lot-r.pdf

Carver, C. S., and M. F. Scheier, "Engagement, Disengagement, Coping, and Catastrophe," in Andrew J. Elliot and Carol S. Dweck, eds., *Handbook of Competence and Motivation*, New York: The Guilford Press, 2005, pp. 527–547.

Carver, C. S., M. F. Scheier, and S. C. Segerstrom, "Optimism," *Clinical Psychology Review*, Vol. 30, No. 7, 2010, pp. 879–889.

Cascio, W. F., "Using Utility Analysis to Assess Training Outcomes," in I. L. Goldstein, ed., *Training and Development in Organizations*, San Francisco: Jossey-Bass, 1989, pp. 63–88.

Cattell, R. B., *Abilities: Their Structure, Growth, and Action*, Boston, Mass.: Houghton-Mifflin, 1971.

Chan, K., and F. Drasgow, "Toward a Theory of Individual Differences and Leadership: Understanding the Motivation to Lead," *Journal of Applied Psychology*, Vol. 86, 2001, pp. 481–498.

Chen, G., S. M. Gully, and D. Eden, "Validation of a New General Self-Efficacy Scale," *Organizational Research Methods*, Vol. 4, 2001, pp. 62–83.

Chen, G., S. M. Gully, J. A. Whiteman, and R. N. Kilcullen, "Examination of Relationships Among Trait-Like Individual Differences, State-Like Individual Differences, and Learning Performance," *Journal of Applied Psychology*, Vol. 85, 2000, pp. 835–847.

Christensen, P. R., P. R. Merrifield, and J. P. Guilford, *Consequences Form A-1*, Beverly Hills, Calif.: Sheridan Supply, 1953.

Clausen, J. A., and M. Gilens, "Personality and Labor Force Participation Across the Life Course: A Longitudinal Study of Women's Careers," *Sociological Forum*, Vol. 5, No. 4, 1990, pp. 595–618.

Cohen, M. S., J. T. Freeman, and S. Wolf, "Metarecognition in Time-Stressed Decision Making: Recognizing, Critiquing, and Correcting," *Human Factors: The Journal of the Human Factors and Ergonomics Society*, Vol. 38, No. 2, 1996, pp. 206–219.

Cohen, M. S., B. B. Thompson, L. Adelman, T. A. Bresnick, L. Shastri, and S. L. Riedel, *Training Critical Thinking for the Battlefield, Volume I: Training System and Evaluation*, Arlington, Va.: U.S. Army Research Institute, Technical Report 00-2, 2000.

Colquitt, J. A., J. A. LePine, and R. A. Noe, "Toward an Integrative Theory of Training Motivation: A Meta-Analytic Path Analysis of 20 Years of Research," *Journal of Applied Psychology*, Vol. 85, No. 5, 2000, pp. 678–707.

Connelly, B. S., and D. S. Ones, "Another Perspective on Personality: Meta-Analytic Integration of Observers' Accuracy and Predictive Validity," *Psychological Bulletin*, Vol. 136, No. 6, 2010, pp. 1092–1122.

Connelly, M. S., J. A. Gilbert, S. J. Zaccaro, K. V. Threlfall, M. A. Marks, and M. D. Mumford, "Exploring the Relationship of Leader Skills and Knowledge to Leader Performance," *Leadership Quarterly*, Vol. 11, No. 1, 2000, pp. 65–86.

Costa, Jr., P. T., and R. R. McCrae, *Revised NEO Personality Inventory (NEO-PI-R) and NEO Five-Factor Inventory (NEOFFI) Professional Manual*, Odessa, Fla.: Psychological Assessment Resources, 1992.

Côté, S., "Emotional Intelligence in Organizations," *Annual Review of Organizational Psychology and Organizational Behavior*, Vol. 1, 2014, pp. 459–488.

Courtright, S. H., B. W. McCormick, B. E. Postlethwaite, C. J. Reeves, and M. K. Mount, "A Meta-Analysis of Sex Differences in Physical Ability: Revised Estimates and Strategies for Reducing Differences in Selection Contexts," *Journal of Applied Psychology*, Vol. 93, No. 4, 2013, pp. 623–641.

Crant, J. M., and T. S. Bateman, "Charismatic Leadership Viewed from Above: The Impact of Proactive Personality," *Journal of Organizational Behavior*, Vol. 21, 2000, pp. 63–75.

Crowne, K. A., "The Relationships Among Social, Emotional, and Cultural Intelligence," *Organizational Management Journal*, Vol. 6, 2009, pp. 148–163.

Dane, E., "Reconsidering the Trade-Off Between Expertise and Flexibility: A Cognitive Entrenchment Perspective," *Academy of Management Review*, Vol. 35, No. 4, 2010, pp. 579–603.

Davidson, J. E., R. Deuser, and R. J. Sternberg, "The Role of Metacognition in Problem Solving," in Janet Metcalfe and Arthur P. Shimamura, eds., *Metacognition: Knowing About Knowing*, Cambridge, Mass.: MIT Press, 1994.

DeRue, D. S., and S. J. Ashford, "Who Will Lead and Who Will Follow? A Social Process of Leadership Identity Construction Organizations," *Academy of Management Review*, Vol. 35, No. 4, 2010, pp. 627–647.

Del Missier, F., T. Mantyla, and W. Bruine de Bruin, "Executive Functions in Decision Making: An Individual Differences Approach," *Thinking and Reasoning*, Vol. 16, No. 2, 2010, pp. 69–97.

Digman, J. M., "Personality Structure: Emergence of the Five-Factor Model," *Annual Review of Psychology*, Vol. 41, 1990, pp. 417–440.

Dirks, K. T., and D. L. Ferrin, "Trust in Leadership: Meta-Analytic Findings and Implications for Research and Practice," *Journal of Applied Psychology*, Vol. 87, No. 4, 2002, pp. 611–628.

Do, M. H., and A. Minbashian, "A Meta-Analytic Examination of the Effects of the Agentic and Affiliative Aspects of Extraversion on Leadership Outcomes," *The Leadership Quarterly*, Vol. 25, 2014, pp. 1040–1053.

Dollinger, S., "Need for Uniqueness, Need for Cognition, and Creativity," *Journal of Creative Behavior*, Vol. 1, No. 37, 2003, pp. 99–116.

Drasgow, F., S. Stark, O. S. Chernyshenko, C. D. Nye, C. L. Hulin, and L. A. White, *Development of the Tailored Adaptive Personality Assessment System (TAPAS) to Support Army Selection and Classification Decisions*, Arlington, Va.: U.S. Army Research Institute for the Behavioral and Social Sciences, Technical Report 1311, 2012.

Duckworth, A. L., C. Peterson, M. D. Matthews, and D. R. Kelly, "Grit: Perseverance and Passion for Long-Term Goals," *Journal of Personality and Social Psychology*, Vol. 92, No. 6, 2007, pp. 1087–1101.

Duckworth, A. L., and P. D. Quinn, "Development and Validation of the Short Grit Scale (Grit-S)," *Journal of Personality Assessment*, Vol. 92, No. 2, 2009, pp. 166–174.

Dudley, N. M., K. A. Orvis, J. E. Lebiecki, and J. M. Cortina, "A Meta-Analytic Investigation of Conscientiousness in the Prediction of Job Performance: Examining the Intercorrelations and the Incremental Validity of Narrow Traits," *Journal of Applied Psychology*, Vol. 91, No. 1, 2006, pp. 40–57.

Dye, D. A., M. Reck, and M. A. McDaniel, "The Validity of Job Knowledge Measures," *International Journal of Selection and Assessment*, Vol. 1, No. 3, 1993, pp. 153–157.

Eden, D., and A. Aviram, "Self-Efficacy Training to Speed Reemployment: Helping People to Help Themselves," *Journal of Applied Psychology*, Vol. 78, 1993, pp. 352–360.

Eisenberger, R., G. Karagonlar, F. Stinglhamber, P. Neves, T. E. Becker, M. G. Gonzalez-Morales, and M. Steiger-Mueller, "Leader–Member Exchange and Affective Organizational Commitment: The Contribution of Supervisor's Organizational Embodiment," *Journal of Applied Psychology*, Vol. 95, No. 6, 2010, pp. 1085–1103.

Endsley, M. R., "Theoretical Underpinnings of Situational Awareness: A Critical Review," in M. R. Endsley and D. J. Garland, eds., *Situation Awareness Analysis and Measurement*, Mahwah, N.J.: Lawrence Erlbaum Associates, 2000, pp. 1–24.

Ennis, R. H., "Critical Thinking Assessment," *Theory into Practice*, Vol. 32, No. 3, 1993, pp. 179–186.

Ennis, R. H., and J. Millman, *Cornell Critical Thinking Test, Level Z*, Pacific Grove, Calif.: Midwest Publications, 2005.

Ennis, R. H., and E. Weir, *The Ennis-Weir Critical Thinking Skills Essay Test*, Pacific Grove, Calif.: Midwest Publications, 1985.

Epitropaki, O., R. Kark, C. Mainemelis, and R. G. Lord, "Leadership and Followership Identity Processes: A Multilevel Review," *The Leadership Quarterly*, 2016. As of December 14, 2016:
http://dx.doi.org/10.1016/j.leaqua.2016.10.003

Ericsson, K. A., "The Influence of Experience and Deliberate Practice on the Development of Superior Expert Performance," in K. A. Ericsson, N. Charness, P. J. Feltovich, and R. R. Hoffman, eds., *The Cambridge Handbook of Expertise and Expert Performance*, New York: Cambridge University Press, 2006, pp. 683–703.

Ericsson, K. A., N. Charness, P. J. Feltovich, and R. R. Hoffman, eds., *The Cambridge Handbook of Expertise and Expert Performance*, New York: Cambridge University Press, 2006.

Ericsson, K. A., R. T. Krampe, and C. Tesch-Romer, "The Role of Deliberate Practice in the Acquisition of Expert Performance," *Psychological Review*, Vol. 100, No. 3, 1993, pp. 363–406.

Eubanks, D. L., S. T. Murphy, and M. D. Mumford, "Intuition as an Influence on Creative Problem-Solving: The Effects of Intuition, Positive Affect, and Training," *Creativity Research Journal*, Vol. 22, No. 2, 2010, pp. 170–184.

Facione, P. A., *The California Critical Thinking Skills Test-College Level, Technical Report #1: Experimental Validation and Content Validity*, Millbrae, Calif.: California Academic Press, 1990.

Ferrando, P. J., and C. Anguiano-Carrasco, "A Structural Model-Based Optimal Person-Fit Procedure for Identifying Faking," *Educational and Psychological Measurement*, Vol. 73, No. 2, 2013, pp. 173–190.

Feuerstein, R., *Instrumental Enrichment: An Intervention Program for Cognitive Modifiability*, Baltimore, Md.: University Park Press, 1980.

Fischer, S. C., V. A. Spiker, D. H. Harris, E. R. McPeters, and S. L. Riedel, *Computerized Training in Critical Thinking (CT): A Skill-Based Program for Army Personnel*, Arlington, Va.: U.S. Army Research Institute for the Behavioral and Social Sciences, Research Report 1880, 2008.

Flavell, J. H., "Metacognition and Cognitive Monitoring: A New Area of Cognitive-Developmental Inquiry," *American Psychologist*, Vol. 34, No. 10, 1979, pp. 906–911.

Flesch, R., "A New Readability Yardstick," *Journal of Applied Psychology*, Vol. 32, No. 3, 1948, p. 221.

Flynn, J. R., "Massive IQ Gains in 14 Nations: What IQ Tests Really Measure," *Psychological Bulletin*, Vol. 101, 1987, pp. 171–191.

Foti, R. J., and N. Hauenstein, "Pattern and Variable Approaches in Leadership Emergence and Effectiveness," *Journal of Applied Psychology*, Vol. 92, No. 2, 2007, pp. 347–355.

Fredrickson, B. L., and T. Joiner, "Positive Emotions Trigger Upward Spirals Toward Emotional Well-Being," *Psychological Science*, Vol. 13, No. 2, 2002, pp. 172–175.

Fredrickson, B. L., M. M. Tugade, C. E. Waugh, and G. R. Larkin, "What Good Are Positive Emotions in Crisis? A Prospective Study of Resilience and Emotions Following the Terrorist Attacks on the United States on September 11th, 2001," *Journal of Personality and Social Psychology*, Vol. 84, No. 2, 2003, pp. 365–376.

Frese, M., "The Word Is Out: We Need an Active Performance Concept for Modern Workplaces," *Industrial and Organizational Psychology*, Vol. 1, 2008, pp. 67–69.

Frese, M., D. Fay, T. Hilburger, K. Leng, and A. Tag, "The Concept of Personal Initiative: Operationalization, Reliability, and Validity in Two German Samples," *Journal of Occupational and Organizational Psychology*, Vol. 70, 1997, pp. 139–161.

Frese, M., W. Kring, A. Soose, and J. Zempel, "Personal Initiative at Work: Differences Between East and West Germany," *Academy of Management Journal*, Vol. 39, No. 1, 1996, pp. 37–63.

Frey, M. C., and D. K. Detterman, "Scholastic Assessment or g? The Relationship Between the Scholastic Assessment Test and General Cognitive Ability," *Psychological Science*, Vol. 15, No. 6, 2004, pp. 373–378.

Gardner, H., *Frames of Mind: The Theory of Multiple Intelligences*, New York: Basic Books, 1993.

Garman, G., *Comparison of Selected Aspects of Personal Initiative Before and After an Initiative Training*, thesis, University of Giessen, 2002.

Geers, A. L., J. A. Wellman, and G. D. Lassiter, "Dispositional Optimism and Engagement: The Moderating Influence of Goal Prioritization," *Journal of Personality and Social Psychology*, Vol. 96, No. 4, 2009, pp. 913–932.

Geiwitz, J., *Training Metacognitive Skills for Problem Solving*, Arlington, Va.: U.S. Army Research Institute for the Behavioral and Social Sciences, Research Note 95-03, 1995.

Gerstner, C. R., and D. V. Day, "Meta-Analytic Review of Leader-Member Exchange Theory: Correlates and Construct Issues," *Journal of Applied Psychology*, Vol. 82, 1997, pp. 827–844.

Glaub, M. E., *Training Personal Initiative to Business Owners in Developing Countries: A Theoretically Derived Intervention and Its Evaluation*, dissertation, University of Vienna, 2009.

Goffin, R. D., and N. D. Christiansen, "Correcting Personality Tests of Faking: A Review of Popular Personality Tests and an Initial Survey of Researchers," *International Journal of Selection and Assessment*, Vol. 11, No. 1/2, 2003, pp. 340–344.

Goldberg, L. R., "A Broad-Bandwidth, Public Domain, Personality Inventory Measuring the Lower-Level Facets of Several Five-Factor Models," in I. Mervielde, I. Deary, F. De Fruyt, and F. Ostendorf, eds., *Personality Psychology in Europe*, Tilburg, The Netherlands: Tilburg University Press, Vol. 7, 1999, pp. 7–28.

Goleman, D., *Emotional Intelligence*, New York: Bantam, 1995.

Goleman, D., and R. Boyatzis, "Social Intelligence and the Biology of Leadership," *Harvard Business Review*, Vol. 86, No. 29, 2008, pp. 74–81.

Gottfredson, L. S., "Mainstream Science on Intelligence: An Editorial with 52 Signatories, History, and Bibliography," *Intelligence*, Vol. 24, 1997, pp. 13–23.

Gottfried, A. E., A. W. Gottfried, R. J. Reichard, D. W. Guerin, P. H. Oliver, and R. E. Riggio, "Motivational Roots of Leadership: A Longitudinal Study from Childhood Through Adulthood," *The Leadership Quarterly*, Vol. 22, No. 3, 2011, pp. 510–519.

Gough, H. G., "A Creative Personality Scale for the Adjective Check List," *Journal of Personality and Social Psychology*, Vol. 37, 1979, pp. 1398–1405.

Gough, H. G., and A. B. Heilbrun, Jr., *The Adjective Check List Manual*, Palo Alto, Calif.: Consulting Psychologists Press, 1965.

Grant, A. M., "Enhancing Coaching Skills and Emotional Intelligence Through Training," *Industrial and Commercial Training*, Vol. 39, No. 5, 2007, pp. 257–266.

Grant, A. M., and J. W. Berry, "The Necessity of Others Is the Mother of Invention: Intrinsic and Prosocial Motivations, Perspective Taking, and Creativity," *Academy of Management Journal*, Vol. 54, 2011, pp. 73–96.

Griffin, M. B., and R. B. McClary, "A Way to Teach Critical Thinking Skills So Learners Will Continue Using Them in Operations," *Military Review*, November–December 2015, pp. 108–118.

Griffith, J., and C. West, "Master Resilience Training and Its Relationship to Individual Well-Being and Stress Buffering Among Army National Guard Soldiers," *The Journal of Behavioral Health Services & Research*, Vol. 40, No. 2, 2013, pp. 140–155.

Griffith, R. L., and M. McDaniel, "The Nature of Deception and Applicant Faking Behavior," in R. L. Griffith and M. H. Peterson, eds., *A Closer Examination of Applicant Faking Behavior*, Information Age Publishing, 2006, pp. 1–19.

Groves, K. S., M. P. McEnrue, and W. Shen, "Developing and Measuring the Emotional Intelligence of Leaders," *Journal of Management Development*, Vol. 22, No. 208, 2006, pp. 225–250.

Guilford, J. P., *The Nature of Human Intelligence*, New York: McGraw-Hill, 1967.

Gustafsson, J. E., "Measurement from a Hierarchical Point of View," in Henry I. Braun, Douglas N. Jackson, and David E. Wiley, eds., *The Role of Construct in Psychological and Educational Measurement*, London: Lawrence-Erlbaum Associates, 2002, pp. 73–95.

Haidt, J., "The Emotional Dog and Its Rational Tail: A Social Intuitionist Approach to Moral Judgment," *Psychological Review*, Vol. 108, No. 4, 2001, pp. 814–834.

Halpern, D. F., "Teaching Critical Thinking for Transfer Across Domains: Dispositions, Skills, Structure Training, and Metacognitive Monitoring," *American Psychologist*, Vol. 53, No. 4, 1998, pp. 449–455.

———, *Halpern Critical Thinking Assessment*, Vienna Test System, Vienna, Austria: Schuhfried, 2010. As of October 15, 2015:
https://www.schuhfried.com/test/HCTA

Hammond, M. M., N. I. Neff, J. L. Farr, A. R. Schwall, and X. Zhao, "Predictors of Individual-Level Innovation at Work: A Meta-Analysis," *Journal of Aesthetics, Creativity, and the Arts*, Vol. 5, 2011, pp. 90–105.

Hannah, S. T., P. A. Balthazard, D. A. Waldman, P. L. Jennings, and R. W. Thatcher, "The Psychological and Neurological Bases of Leader Self-Complexity and Effects on Adaptive Decision-Making," *Journal of Applied Psychology*, Vol. 98, No. 3, 2013, pp. 393–411.

Harms, P. D., and M. Credé, "Emotional Intelligence and Transformational and Transactional Leadership: A Meta-Analysis," *Journal of Leadership & Organizational Studies*, Vol. 17, No. 1, 2010, pp. 5–17.

Harrison, J. K., M. Chadwick, and M. Scales, "The Relationship Between Cross-Cultural Adjustment and the Personality Variables of Self-Efficacy and Self-Monitoring," *International Journal of Intercultural Relations*, Vol. 20, 1996, pp. 167–188.

Harrison, T. L., Z. Shipstead, K. L. Hicks, D. Z. Hambrick, T. S. Redick, and R. W. Engle, "Working Memory Training May Increase Working Memory Capacity but Not Fluid Intelligence," *Psychological Science*, Vol. 24, No. 12, 2013, pp. 2409–2419.

Headquarters, Department of the Army, *Army Physical Readiness Training*, Field Manual (FM) 7-22, C1, Washington, D.C.: May 2012a.

———, *Army Leadership*, ADRP 6-22, C1, Washington, D.C.: September 2012b.

———, *Leader Development*, Field Manual (FM) 6-22, Washington, D.C.: June 2015.

Hedlund, J., G. B. Forsythe, J. A. Horvath, W. M. Williams, S. Snook, and R. J. Sternberg, "Identifying and Assessing Tacit Knowledge: Understanding the Practical Intelligence of Military Leaders," *The Leadership Quarterly*, Vol. 14, 2003, pp. 117–140.

Helson, R., S. Y. V. Kwan, O. P. John, and C. Jones, "The Growing Evidence for Personality Change in Adulthood: Findings from Research with Personality Inventories," *Journal of Research in Personality*, Vol. 36, No. 4, 2002, pp. 287–306.

Hocevar, D., "The Development of the Creative Behavior Inventory (CBI)," Rocky Mountain Psychological Association Annual Meeting, April 1979.

Hoever, I. J., D. van Knippenberg, W. P. van Ginkel, and H. G. Barkema, "Fostering Team Creativity: Perspective Taking as Key to Unlocking Diversity's Potential," *Journal of Applied Psychology*, Vol. 97, 2012, pp. 982–996.

Hogan, J., "Personality Correlates of Physical Fitness," *Journal of Personality and Social Psychology*, Vol. 56, No.2, 1989, pp. 284–288.

———, "Structure of Physical Performance in Occupational Tasks," *Journal of Applied Psychology*, Vol. 76, No. 4, August 1991, pp. 495–507.

Hogan, R. T., and J. Hogan, *Manual for the Hogan Personality Inventory* (2nd ed.), Hogan Assessment Systems, Tulsa, Okla.: 1995.

Holyoak, K. J., "Symbolic Connectionism: Toward Third-Generation Theories of Expertise," in K. A. Ericsson and J. Smith, eds., *Toward a General Theory of Expertise: Prospects and Limits*, New York: Cambridge University Press, 1991, pp. 301–335.

Hong, Y., V. M. Catano, and H. Liao, "Leader Emergence: The Role of Emotional Intelligence and Motivation to Lead," *Leadership & Organization Development Journal*, Vol. 32, No. 4, 2011, pp. 320–343.

Hooijberg, R., J. G. Hunt, and G. E. Dodge, "Leadership Complexity and Development of the Leaderplex Model," *Journal of Management*, Vol. 23, 1997, pp. 375–408.

Horn, J., and H. Masunaga, "A Merging Theory of Expertise and Intelligence," in K. A. Ericsson, N. Charness, P. J. Feltovich, and R. R. Hoffman, eds., *The Cambridge Handbook of Expertise and Expert Performance*, New York: Cambridge University Press, 2006, pp. 587–611.

Huffcutt, A. I., and W. Arthur, "Hunter and Hunter (1984) Revisited: Interview Validity for Entry-Level Jobs," *Journal of Applied Psychology*, Vol. 79, 1994, pp. 184–190.

Huffcutt, A. I., J. M. Conway, P. L. Roth, and N. J. Stone, "Identification and Meta-Analytic Assessment of Psychological Constructs Measured in Employment Interviews," *Journal of Applied Psychology*, Vol. 86, No. 5, 2001, pp. 897–913.

Hunter, J. E., and R. F. Hunter, "Validity and Utility of Alternative Predictors of Job Performance," *Psychological Bulletin*, Vol. 96, No. 1, 1984, pp. 72–98.

"International Personality Item Pool," webpage, last updated February 22, 2017. As of September 12, 2015:
http://ipip.ori.org

Jacobs, T. O., and E. Jaques, "Leadership in Complex Systems," in J. Zeidner, ed., *Human Productivity Enhancement*, New York: Praeger, 1987, pp. 7–65.

Jacobson, R. "Teachers Improving Learning Using Metacognition with Self-Monitoring Learning Strategies," *Education*, 1998, pp. 579–589.

Jaeggi, S. M., M. Buschkuehl, J. Jonides, and W. J. Perrig, "Improving Fluid Intelligence with Training on Working Memory," *Proceedings of the National Academy of Sciences of the United States of America*, Vol. 105, 2008, pp. 6829–6833.

Jaeggi, S. M., M. Buschkuehl, P. Shah, and J. Jonides, "The Role of Individual Differences in Cognitive Training and Transfer," *Memory & Cognition*, Vol. 42, No. 3, 2014, pp. 464–480.

Jensen, A. R., *The g Factor: The Science of Mental Ability*, Westport, Conn.: Praeger, 1998.

Johnson, D. C., N. J. Thom, E. A. Stanley, L. Haase, A. N. Simmons, P. B. Shih, W. K. Thompson, E. G. Potterat, T. R. Minor, and M. P. Paulus, "Modifying Resilience Mechanisms in At-Risk Individuals: A Controlled Study of Mindfulness Training in Marines Preparing for Deployment," *American Journal of Psychiatry*, Vol. 171, No. 8, 2014, pp. 844–853.

Jones, T. M., "Ethical Decision Making by Individuals in Organizations: An Issue-Contingent Model," *Academy of Management Review*, Vol. 16, No. 2, 1991, pp. 366–395.

Joseph, D. L., J. Jin, D. A. Newman, and E. H. O'Boyle, "Why Does Self-Reported Emotional Intelligence Predict Job Performance? A Meta-Analytic Investigation of Mixed EI," *Journal of Applied Psychology*, Vol. 100, No. 2, 2015, pp. 298–342.

Joseph, D. L., and D. A. Newman, "Emotional Intelligence: An Integrative Meta-Analysis and Cascading Model," *Journal of Applied Psychology*, Vol. 95, 2010, pp. 54–78.

Judge, T. A., and J. E. Bono, "Relationship of Core Self-Evaluations Traits—Self-Esteem, Generalized Self-Efficacy, Locus of Control, and Emotional Stability—with Job Satisfaction and Job Performance: A Meta-Analysis," *Journal of Applied Psychology*, Vol. 86, No. 1, 2001, pp. 80–92.

Judge, T. A., J. E. Bono, R. Ilies, and M. W. Gerhardt, "Personality and Leadership: A Qualitative and Quantitative Review," *Journal of Applied Psychology*, Vol. 87, No. 4, 2002, pp. 765–780.

Judge, T. A., A. E. Colbert, and R. Ilies, "Intelligence and Leadership: A Quantitative Review and Test of Theoretical Propositions," *Journal of Applied Psychology*, Vol. 89, No. 3, 2004, pp. 542–552.

Judge, T. A., C. A. Higgins, C. J. Thoresen, and M. R. Barrick, "The Big Five Personality Traits, General Mental Ability, and Career Success Across the Life Span," *Personnel Psychology*, Vol. 52, 1999, pp. 621–652.

Judge, T. A., and C. P. Zapata, "The Person-Situation Debate Revisited: Effect of Situation Strength and Trait Activation on the Validity of the Big Five Personality Traits in Predicting Job Performance," *Academy of Management Journal*, Vol. 58, No. 4, 2015, pp. 1149–1179.

Kahneman, D., and G. Klein, "Conditions for Intuitive Expertise: A Failure to Disagree," *American Psychologist*, Vol. 64, No. 6, 2009, pp. 515–526.

Kahneman, D., and A. Tversky, "Subjective Probability: A Judgment of Representativeness," *Cognitive Psychology*, Vol. 3, No. 3, 1972, pp. 430–454.

Kark, R., and D. Van Dijk, "Motivation to Lead, Motivation to Follow: The Role of the Self Regulatory Focus in Leadership Processes," *Academy of Management Review*, Vol. 32, No. 2, 2007, pp. 500–528.

Karrasch, A. I., "Antecedents and Consequences of Organizational Commitment," *Military Psychology*, Vol. 15, 2003, pp. 225–236.

Katz, D., and R. L. Kahn, *The Social Psychology of Organizations* (2nd ed.), New York: John Wiley and Sons, 1978.

Kaufman, J. C., J. C. Cole, and J. Baer, "The Construct of Creativity: A Structural Model for Self-Reported Creativity Ratings," *Journal of Creative Behavior*, Vol. 43, No. 2, 2009, pp. 119–134.

Kelly, D. R., M. D. Matthews, and P. T. Bartone, "Grit and Hardiness as Predictors of Performance among West Point Cadets," *Military Psychology*, Vol. 26, No. 4, 2014, pp. 327–342.

Kimball, D. R., and K. J. Holyoak, "Transfer and Expertise," *The Oxford Handbook of Memory*, 2000, pp. 109–122.

Kirby, E. G., S. L. Kirby, and M. A. Lewis, "A Study of the Effectiveness of Training Proactive Thinking," *Journal of Applied Social Psychology*, Vol. 32, 2002, pp. 1538–1549.

Kish-Gephart, J. J., D. A. Harrison, and L. Klebe Treviño, "Bad Apples, Bad Cases, and Bad Barrels: Meta-Analytic Evidence About Sources of Unethical Decisions at Work," *Journal of Applied Psychology*, Vol. 95, No. 1, 2010, pp. 1–31.

Klaczynski, P. A., D. H. Gordon, and J. Fauth, "Goal-Oriented Critical Reasoning and Individual Differences in Critical Reasoning Biases," *Journal of Educational Psychology*, Vol. 89, No. 3, 1997, pp. 470–485.

Knapik, J. J., M. A. Sharp, S. Darakjy, S. B. Jones, K. G. Hauret, and B. H. Jones, "Temporal Changes in the Physical Fitness of U.S. Army Recruits," *Sports Medicine*, Vol. 36, No. 7, November 2006, pp. 613–634.

Kobasa, S. C., "Stressful Life Events, Personality, and Health: An Inquiry into Hardiness," *Journal of Personality and Social Psychology*, Vol. 37, 1979, pp. 1–11.

Kobasa, S. C., S. R. Maddi, and S. Kahn, "Hardiness and Health: A Prospective Study," *Journal of Personality and Social Psychology*, Vol. 42, 1982, pp. 168–177.

Kobe, L. M., R. Reiter-Palmon, and J. D. Rickers, "Self-Reported Leadership Experiences in Relation to Inventoried Social and Emotional Intelligence," *Current Psychology: Developmental, Learning, Personality, Social*, Vol. 20, 2001, pp. 154–163.

Koenig, K. A., M. C. Frey, and D. K. Detterman, "ACT and General Cognitive Ability," *Intelligence*, Vol. 36, 2008, pp. 153–160.

Kohlberg, L., "Stage and Sequence: The Cognitive Developmental Approach to Socialization," in D. A. Goslin, ed., *Handbook of Socialization Theory and Research*, Chicago, Ill.: Rand McNally, 1969, pp. 347–480.

Kraemer, W. J., N. A. Ratamess, and D. N. French, "Resistance Training for Health and Performance," *Current Sports Medicine Reports*, Vol. 1, 2002, pp. 165–171.

Ku, K. Y. L., "Assessing Students' Critical Thinking Performance: Urging for Measurements Using Multi-Response Format," *Thinking Skills and Creativity*, Vol. 4, No. 1, 2009, pp. 70–76.

Kvist, A. V., and J. E. Gustafsson, "The Relation Between Fluid Intelligence and the General Factor as a Function of Cultural Background: A Test of Cattell's Investment Theory," *Intelligence*, Vol. 36, No. 5, 2008, pp. 422–436.

Lai, E. R., "Metacognition: A Literature Review," *Always Learning: Pearson Research Report*, 2011. As of December 28, 2016:
http://images.pearsonassessments.com/images/tmrs/metacognition_literature_review_final.pdf

Landy, F. J., "Some Historical and Scientific Issues Related to Research on Emotional Intelligence," *Journal of Organizational Behavior*, Vol. 26, 2005, pp. 411–424.

———, "The Long, Frustrating, and Fruitless Search for Social Intelligence: A Cautionary Tale," in K. R. Murphy, ed., *A Critique of Emotional Intelligence: What Are the Problems and How Can They Be Fixed?* Mahwah, N.J.: Lawrence Erlbaum Associates Publishers, 2006, pp. 81–123.

Legree, P. J., R. N. Kilcullen, D. J. Putka, and L. E. Wasko, "Identifying the Leaders of Tomorrow: Validating Predictors of Leader Performance," *Military Psychology*, Vol. 26, 2014, pp. 292–309.

Lievens, F., and B. De Soete, "Simulations," in N. Schmitt, ed., *The Oxford Handbook of Personnel Assessment and Selection*, New York: Oxford University Press, 2012, pp. 383–410.

Lord, R. G., C. L. De Vader, and G. M. Alliger, "A Meta-Analysis of the Relation between Personality Traits and Leadership Perceptions: An Application of Validity Generalization Procedures," *Journal of Applied Psychology*, Vol. 71, 1986, pp. 402–410.

Lucas, K. W., and J. Markessini, *CAE-LINK Corporation, Senior Leadership in a Changing World Order: Requisite Skills for U.S. Army One-and Two-Star Assignments*, Alexandria, Va.: U.S. Army Research Institute for the Behavioral and Social Science, Technical Report 976, 1993.

Luthans, F., J. B. Avey, and J. L. Patera, "Experimental Analysis of a Web-Based Training Intervention to Develop Positive Psychological Capital," *Academy of Management Learning & Education*, Vol. 7, No. 2, 2008, pp. 209–221.

Luthans, F., and C. M. Youssef, "Emerging Positive Organizational Behavior," *Journal of Management*, Vol. 33, No. 3, 2007, pp. 321–349.

Maddi, S. R., "Relevance of Hardiness Assessment and Training to the Military Context," *Military Psychology*, Vol. 19, 2007, pp. 61–70.

Maddi, S. R., R. H. Harvey, D. M. Khoshaba, M. Fazel, and N. Resurreccion, "Personality Construct of Hardiness, IV: Positive Cognitions and Emotions Concerning Oneself and Developmentally Relevant Activities," *Journal of Humanistic Psychology*, 2009, pp. 1–14.

Maddi, S. R., M. D. Matthews, D. R. Kelly, N. Resurreccion, and B. J. Villarreal, "The Relationship Between Hardiness and Performance in Challenging Environments," Presentation at the 118th American Psychological Association Convention, San Diego, Calif., August 2010.

Maddi, S. R., M. D. Matthews, D. R. Kelly, B. Villarreal, and M. White, "The Role of Hardiness and Grit in Predicting Performance and Retention of USMA Cadets," *Military Psychology*, Vol. 24, No. 1, 2012, pp. 19–28.

Marshall-Mies, J. C., E. A. Fleishmab, J. A. Martic, S. J. Zaccaro, W. A. Baughman, and M. L. McGee, "Development and Evaluation of Cognitive and Metacognitive Measures for Predicting Leadership Potential," *The Leadership Quarterly*, Vol. 11, No. 1, 2000, pp. 135–153.

Martin, K. D., and J. B. Cullen, "Continuities and Extensions of Ethical Climate Theory: A Meta-Analytic Review," *Journal of Business Ethics*, Vol. 69, No. 2, 2006, pp. 175–194.

Martin, M. M., and C. M. Anderson, "The Cognitive Flexibility Scale: Three Validity Studies," *Communication Reports*, Vol. 11, No. 1, 1998, pp. 1–9.

Martin, M. M., and R. B. Rubin, "A New Measure of Cognitive Flexibility," *Psychological Reports*, Vol. 76, No. 2, 1995, pp. 623–626.

Matthews, M. D., *Head Strong: How Psychology Is Revolutionizing War*, New York: Oxford University Press, 2014.

Mayer, J. D., R. D. Roberts, and S. G. Barsade, "Human Abilities: Emotional Intelligence," *Annual Review of Psychology*, Vol. 59, 2008, pp. 507–536.

Mayer, J. D., and P. Salovey, "The Intelligence of Emotional Intelligence," *Intelligence*, Vol. 17, No. 4, 1993,.pp. 433–442.

———, "What Is Emotional Intelligence?" in P. Salovey and D. Sluyter, eds., *Emotional Development and Emotional Intelligence: Implications for Educators*, New York: Basic Books, 1997, pp. 3–34.

Mayer, J. D., P. Salovey, D. R. Caruso, and G. Sitarenios, "Measuring Emotional Intelligence with the MSCEIT V2.0," *Emotion*, Vol. 3, No. 1, 2003, pp. 97–105.

McArdle W. D., F. I. Katch, and V. L. Katch, *Exercise Physiology: Energy, Nutrition and Human Performance*, Philadelphia, Pa.: Lea & Febiger, 1991.

McCabe, J., "Metacognitive Awareness of Learning Strategies in Undergraduates," *Memory and Cognition*, Vol. 39, 2011, pp. 462–476.

McCrae, R. R., and P. T. Costa, Jr., "A Contemplated Revision of the NEO Five-Factor Inventory," *Personality and Individual Differences*, Vol. 36, 2004, pp. 587–596.

McDaniel, M. A., F. L. Schmidt, and J. E. Hunter, "Job Experience Correlates of Job Performance," *Journal of Applied Psychology*, Vol. 73, 1988, pp. 327–330.

Mencl, J., L. Tay, C. E. Schwoerer, and F. Drasgow, "Evaluating Quantitative and Qualitative Types of Change: An Analysis of the Malleability of General and Specific Self-Efficacy Constructs and Measures," *Journal of Leadership and Organizational Studies*, Vol. 19, 2012, pp. 379–391.

Meredith, L. S., C. S. Sims, B. S. Batorsky, A. Okunogbe, B. L. Bannon, and C. A. Myatt, *Identifying Promising Approaches to US Army Institutional Change*. Santa Monica, Calif.: RAND Corporation, RR-1588-A, 2017. As of February 13, 2018: https://www.rand.org/pubs/research_reports/RR1588.html

Mesmer-Magnus, J. R., and C. Viswesvaran, "Whistleblowing in Organizations: An Examination of Correlates of Whistleblowing Intentions, Actions, and Retaliation," *Journal of Business Ethics*, Vol. 62, No. 3, 2005, pp. 277–297.

Meyer, J. P., N. J. Allen, and C. A. Smith, "Commitment to Organizations and Occupations: Extension and Test of a Three-Component Conceptualization," *Journal of Applied Psychology*, Vol. 78, No. 4, 1993, pp. 538–551.

Meyer, J. P., D. J. Stanley, L. Herscovitch, and L. Topolnytsky, "Affective, Continuance, and Normative Commitment to the Organization: A Meta-Analysis of Antecedents, Correlates, and Consequences," *Journal of Vocational Behavior*, Vol. 61, 2002, pp. 20–52.

Mills, L. B., "A Meta-Analysis of the Relationship Between Emotional Intelligence and Effective Leadership," *Journal of Curriculum and Instruction*, Vol. 3, No. 2, 2009, pp. 22–38.

Moritz, S., R. Veckenstedt, S. Randjbar, F. Vitzthum, and T. S. Woodward, "Antipsychotic Treatment Beyond Antipsychotics: Metacognitive Intervention for Schizophrenia Patients Improves Delusional Symptoms," *Psychological Medicine*, Vol. 41, 2011, pp. 1823–1832.

Morrison, E. W., and C. C. Phelps, "Taking Charge at Work: Extrarole Efforts to Initiate Workplace Change," *Academy of Management Journal*, Vol. 42, No. 4, 1999, pp. 403–419.

Mowday, R. T., R. M. Steers, and L. W. Porter, "The Measurement of Organizational Commitment," *Journal of Vocational Behavior*, Vol. 14, 1979, pp. 224–247.

Mueller-Hanson, R. A., S. S. White, D. W. Dorsey, and E. D. Pulakos, *Training Adaptable Leaders: Lessons from Research and Practice*, Arlington, Va.: U.S. Army Research Institute for Behavioral and Social Sciences, Research Report 1844, 2005.

Mumford, M. D., M. A. Campion, and F. P. Morgeson, "The Leadership Skills Strataplex: Leadership Skill Requirements across Organizational Levels," *The Leadership Quarterly*, Vol. 18, 2007, pp. 154–166.

Mumford, M. D., S. Connelly, R. P. Brown, S. T. Murphy, J. H. Hill, A. L. Antes, E. P. Waples, and L. D. Devenport, "A Sensemaking Approach to Ethics Training for Scientists: Preliminary Evidence of Training Effectiveness," *Ethics & Behavior*, Vol. 18, No. 4, 2008, pp. 315–339.

Mumford, M. D., S. Connelly, and B. Gaddis, "How Creative Leaders Think: Experimental Findings and Cases," *The Leadership Quarterly*, Vol. 14, 2003, pp. 411–432.

Mumford, M. D., M. I. Mobley, R. Reiter-Palmon, C. E. Uhlman, and L. M. Doares, "Process Analytic Models of Creative Capacities," *Creativity Research Journal*, Vol. 4, No. 2, 1991, pp. 91–122.

Nelis, D., J. Quoidbach, M. Mikolajczak, and M. Hansenne, "Increasing Emotional Intelligence: (How) Is It Possible?" *Personality and Individual Differences*, Vol. 47, 2009, pp. 36–41.

Nelson, J. K., S. J. Zaccaro, and J. L. Herman, "Strategic Information Provision and Experiential Variety as Tools for Developing Adaptive Leadership Skills," *Consulting Psychology Journal: Practice and Research*, Vol. 62, No. 2, 2010, pp. 131–142.

Nindl, B. C., B. A. Alvar, J. R. Dudley, M. W. Favre, G. J. Martin, M. A. Sharp, B. J. Warr, M. D. Stephenson, and W. J. Kraemer, "Executive Summary from the National Strength and Conditioning Association's Second Blue Ribbon Panel on Military Physical Readiness: Military Physical Performance Testing," *Journal of Strength and Conditioning Research*, Vol. 29, 2015, pp. S216–S220.

North Atlantic Treaty Organization Research and Technology Organization, *Optimizing Operational Physical Fitness*, RTO Technical Report TF-HRM-080, 2009.

Nye, C. E., F. Drasgow, O. S. Chernyshenko, S. Stark, U. C. Kubisiak, L. A. White, and I. Jose, *Assessing the Tailored Adaptive Personality Assessment System (TAPAS) as an MOS Qualification Instrument*, Arlington, Va.: U.S. Army Research Institute for the Behavioral and Social Sciences, Technical Report 1312, 2012.

O'Boyle, E. H., R. H. Humphrey, J. M. Pollack, T. H. Hawver, and P. A. Story, "The Relation between Emotional Intelligence and Job Performance: A Meta-Analysis," *Journal of Organizational Behavior*, Vol. 32, 2011, pp. 788–818.

O'Fallon, M. J., and K. D. Butterfield, "A Review of the Empirical Ethical Decision-Making Literature: 1996–2003," *Journal of Business Ethics*, Vol. 59, No. 4, 2005, pp. 375–413.

Olsen, O. K., J. Eid, and B. H. Johnsen, "Moral Behavior and Transformational Leadership in Norwegian Naval Cadets," *Military Psychology*, Vol. 18, 2006, pp. S37–S56.

Ones, D. S., S. Dilchert, C. Viswesvaran, and J. F. Salgado, "Cognitive Abilities," in J. L. Farr and N. T. Tippins, eds., *Handbook of Employee Selection*, New York: Routledge/Taylor & Francis Group, 2010, pp. 255–275.

O'Reilly, C. A., and J. Chatman, "Organizational Commitment and Psychological Attachment: The Effects of Compliance, Identification, and Internalization on Prosocial Behavior," *Journal of Applied Psychology*, Vol. 71, No. 3, 1986, pp. 492–499.

Parker, A. M., W. Bruine de Bruin, and B. Fischhoff, "Maximizers versus Satisfiers: Decision-Making Styles, Competence, and Outcomes," *Judgment and Decision Making*, Vol. 2, No. 6, 2007, pp. 342–350.

Parker, S. K., and C. M. Axtell, "Seeing Another Viewpoint: Antecedents and Outcomes of Employee Perspective Taking," *Academy of Management Journal*, Vol. 44, 2001, pp. 1085–1100.

Pearson Assessment, "Miller Analogies Test (MAT)," webpage, 2016. As of February 2, 2016:
http://www.pearsonassessments.com/postsecondaryeducation/graduate_admissions/mat.html

Petrides, K. V., and A. Furnham, "Trait Emotional Intelligence: Psychometric Investigation with Reference to Established Trait Taxonomies," *European Journal of Personality*, Vol. 15, 2001, pp. 425–448.

Phillips, J. K., G. Klein, and W. R. Sieck, "Expertise in Judgment and Decision Making: A Case for Training Intuitive Decision Skills," in D. J. Koehler and N. Harvey, eds., *Blackwell Handbook of Judgment and Decision Making*, Malden, Mass.: Blackwell Publishing, 2004, pp. 297–315.

Pintrich, P. R., D. A. F. Smith, T. Garcia, and W. J. McKeachie, "Reliability and Validity of the Motivated Strategies for Learning Questionnaire (MSLQ)," *Educational and Psychological Measurement*, Vol. 53, 1993, pp. 801–813.

Pleban, R. J., J. S. Tucker, V. Johnson, K. Gunther, and T. R. Graves, *Training Situation Awareness and Adaptive Decision-Making Skills Using a Desktop Computer Simulation*, Arlington, Va.: U.S. Army Research Institute for the Behavioral and Social Sciences, Research Report 1889, 2009, pp. 1–58.

Plomin, R., and J. C. DeFries, "The Genetics of Cognitive Abilities and Disabilities," *Scientific American*, Vol. 278, No. 5, 1998, pp. 62–69.

Pulakos, E. D., S. Arad, M. A. Donovan, and K. E. Plamondon, "Adaptability in the Workplace: Development of a Taxonomy of Adaptive Performance," *Journal of Applied Psychology*, Vol. 85, No. 4, 2000, pp. 612–624.

Pulakos, E. D., N. Schmitt, D. W. Dorsey, S. Arad, J. W. Hedge, and W. C. Borman, "Predicting Adaptive Performance: Further Tests of a Model of Adaptability," *Human Performance*, Vol. 15, No. 4, 2002, pp. 299–323.

Quiñones, M. A., J. K. Ford, and M. S. Teachout, "The Relationship Between Work Experience and Job Performance: A Conceptual and Meta-Analytic Review," *Personnel Psychology*, Vol. 48, No. 4, 1995, pp. 887–910.

Raven, J., J. C. Raven, and J. H. Court, *Manual for Raven's Progressive Matrices and Vocabulary Scales*, Oxford: Oxford Psychologists Press, 1998.

Rees, B., "Overview of Outcome Data for Potential Mediation Training for Soldier Resilience," *Military Medicine*, Vol. 176, No. 11, 2011, pp. 1232–1242.

Rest, J. R., *Moral Development: Advances in Research and Theory*, New York: Praeger, 1986a.

———, *DIT Manual for the Defining Issues Test*, Minneapolis, Minn.: University of Minnesota Center for the Study of Ethical Development, 1986b.

Rest, J. R., D. Narvaez, M. J. Bebeau, and S. J. Thoma, "Neo-Kohlbergian Approach: The DIT and the Schema Theory," *Educational Psychology Review*, Vol. 11, No. 4, 1999, pp. 291–324.

Reynolds, S. J., "A Neurocognitive Model of the Ethical Decision-Making Process: Implications for Study and Practice," *Journal of Applied Psychology*, Vol. 91, 2006, pp. 737–748.

Rice, R. W., J. D. Yoder, J. Adams, R. F. Priest, and H. T. Prince, "Leadership Ratings for Male and Female Military Cadets," *Sex Roles*, Vol. 10, 1984, pp. 885–901.

Riggio, R. E., and R. J. Reichard, "The Emotional and Social Intelligences of Effective Leadership," *Journal of Managerial Psychology*, Vol. 23, No. 2, 2008, pp. 169–185.

Riketta, M., "Attitudinal Organizational Commitment and Job Performance: A Meta-Analysis," *Journal of Organizational Behavior*, Vol. 23, 2002, pp. 257–266.

Roberts, B. W., "Plaster or Plasticity: Are Adult Work Experiences Associated with Personality Changes in Women?" *Journal of Personality*, Vol. 65, 1997, pp. 205–232.

Roberts, B. W., A. Caspi, and T. E. Moffitt, "Work Experiences and Personality Development in Young Adulthood," *Journal of Personality and Social Psychology*, Vol. 84, No. 3, 2003, pp. 582–593.

Roberts, B. W., O. S. Chernyshenko, S. Stark, and L. Goldberg, "The Construct of Conscientiousness: The Convergence Between Lexical Models and Scales Drawn from Six Major Personality Questionnaires," *Personnel Psychology*, Vol. 58, 2005, pp. 103–139.

Roberts, B. W., K. E. Walton, and W. Viechtbauer, "Patterns of Mean-Level Change in Personality Traits Across the Life Course: A Meta-Analysis of Longitudinal Studies," *Psychological Bulletin*, Vol. 132, 2006, pp. 1–25.

Robson, S., *Physical Fitness and Resilience: A Review of Relevant Constructs, Measures, and Links to Well-Being*, Santa Monica, Calif.: RAND Corporation, RR-104-AF, 2013. As of January 3, 2017: https://www.rand.org/pubs/research_reports/RR104.html

Rueb, J. D., H. J. Erskine, and R. I. Foti, "Intelligence, Dominance, Masculinity, and Self-Monitoring: Predicting Leadership Emergence in a Military Setting," *Military Psychology*, Vol. 20, 2008, pp. 237–252.

Salgado, J. F., N. Anderson, S. Moscoso, C. Bertua, and F. de Fruyt, "International Validity Generalization of GMA and Cognitive Abilities: A European Community Meta-Analysis," *Personnel Psychology*, Vol. 56, 2006, pp. 573–605.

Salgado, J. F., S. Moscoso, and P. Alonso, "Subdimensional Structure of the Hogan Personality Inventory," *International Journal of Selection and Assessment*, Vol. 21, No. 3, 2013, pp. 277–285.

Salovey, P., and J. D. Mayer, "Emotional Intelligence," *Imagination, Cognition, and Personality*, Vol. 9, No. 3, 1990, pp. 185–211.

Salthouse, T., "Consequences of Age-Related Cognitive Declines," *Annual Review of Psychology*, Vol. 63, 2012, pp. 201–226.

Saus, E. R., B. H. Johnsen, J. Eid, P. K. Riisem, R. Andersen, and J. F. Thayer, "The Effect of Brief Situational Awareness Training in a Police Shooting Simulator: An Experimental Study," *Military Psychology*, Vol. 18, Suppl. 1, 2006, pp. 3–21.

Scheier, M. F., and C. S. Carver, "Optimism, Coping, and Health: Assessment and Implications of Generalized Outcome Expectancies," *Health Psychology*, Vol. 4, No. 3, 1985, pp. 219–247.

Scheier, M. F., C. S. Carver, and M. S. Bridges, "Distinguishing Optimism from Neuroticism (and Trait Anxiety, Self-Mastery, and Self-Esteem): A Reevaluation of the Life Orientation Test," *Journal of Personality and Social Psychology*, Vol. 67, No. 6, 1994, pp. 1063–1078.

Schein, E. H., "Organizational Culture," *American Psychologist*, Vol. 45, No. 2, 1990, pp. 109–119.

———, *Organizational Culture and Leadership*, 3rd ed., San Francisco, Calif.: John Wiley & Sons, 2004.

Scherbaum, C. A., Y. Cohen-Charash, and M. J. Kern, "Measuring General Self-Efficacy: A Comparison of Three Measures Using Item Response Theory," *Educational and Psychological Measurement*, Vol. 66, No. 6, 2006, pp. 1047–1063.

Schleicher, D. J., S. D. Hansen, and K. E. Fox, "Job Attitudes and Work Values," in S. Zedeck, ed., *APA Handbook of Industrial and Organizational Psychology*, Washington, D.C.: American Psychological Association, 2011, pp. 137–189.

Schmidt, A. M., and J. K. Ford, "Learning Within a Learner Control Training Environment: The Interactive Effects of Goal Orientation and Metacognitive Instruction on Learning Outcomes," *Personnel Psychology*, Vol. 56, 2003, pp. 405–429.

Schmidt, F. L., "The Role of General Cognitive Ability and Job Performance: Why There Cannot be a Debate," *Human Performance*, Vol. 15, No. 1–2, 2002, pp. 187–210.

Schmidt, F. L., and J. E. Hunter, "Development of a Causal Model of Processes Determining Job Performance," *Current Directions in Psychological Science*, Vol. 1, No. 3, 1992, pp. 89–92.

———, "The Validity and Utility of Selection Methods in Personnel Psychology: Practical and Theoretical Implications of 85 Years of Research Findings," *Psychological Bulletin*, Vol. 124, No. 2, 1998, pp. 262–274.

———, "General Mental Ability in the World of Work: Occupational Attainment and Job Performance," *Journal of Personality and Social Psychology*, Vol. 86, No. 1, 2004, pp. 162–173.

Schmidt, F. L., J. E. Hunter, and K. Pearlman, "Assessing the Economic Impact of Personnel Programs on Workforce Productivity," *Personnel Psychology*, Vol. 35, No. 2, 1982, pp. 333–347.

Schmiedek, F., M. Lövdén, and U. Lindenberger, "Younger Adults Show Long-Term Effects of Cognitive Training on Broad Cognitive Abilities Over 2 Years," *Developmental Psychology*, Vol. 50, No. 9, 2014, pp. 2304–2310.

Schraw, G., "Promoting General Metacognitive Awareness," *Instructional Science*, Vol. 25, 1998, pp. 113–125.

Schraw, G., and R. S. Dennison, "Assessing Metacognitive Awareness," *Contemporary Educational Psychology*, Vol. 19, 1994, pp. 460–475.

Schwarzer, R., and M. Jerusalem, "Generalized Self-Efficacy Scale," in J. Weinman, S. C. Wright, and M. Johnston, eds., *Measures in Health Psychology: A User's Portfolio: Causal and Control Beliefs*, Windsor, U.K.: NFER-Nelson, 1995, pp. 35–37.

Schwoerer, C. E., D. R. May, E. C. Hollensbe, and J. Mencl, "General and Specific Self-Efficacy in the Context of a Training Intervention to Enhance Performance Expectancy," *Human Resource Development Quarterly*, Vol. 16, No. 1, 2005, pp. 111–129.

Scott, G., L. E. Leritz, and M. D. Mumford, "The Effectiveness of Creativity Training: A Quantitative Review," *Creativity Research Journal*, Vol. 16, No. 4, 2004, pp. 361–288.

Scott, G. M., D. C. Lonergan, and M. D. Mumford, "Conceptual Combination: Alternative Knowledge Structures, Alternative Heuristics," *Creativity Research Journal*, Vol. 17, No. 1, 2005, pp. 79–98.

Seiler, S., A. Fischer, and Y. P. Ooi, "An Interactional Dual-Process Model of Moral Decision Making Guide to Military Training," *Military Psychology*, Vol. 22, 2010, pp. 490–509.

Seligman, M. E. P., "Building Human Strength: Psychology's Forgotten Mission," *APA Monitor*, Vol. 29, No. 1, 1998, p. 2.

Shakeshaft, N. G., M. Trzaskowski, A. McMillan, E. Krapohl, M. A. Simpson, A. Reichenberg, M. Cederlöf, H. Larsson, P. Lichtenstein, and R. Plomin, "Thinking Positively: The Genetics of High Intelligence," *Intelligence*, Vol. 48, 2015, pp. 123–132.

Shanteau, J., "Competence in Experts: The Role of Task Characteristics," *Organizational Behavior and Human Decision Processes*, Vol. 53, No. 2, 1992, pp. 252–266.

Sharp, M. A., *Physical Fitness, Physical Training, and Occupational Performance of Men and Women in the U.S. Army: A Review of the Literature*, U.S. Army Research Institute of Environmental Medicine, Technical Note 93-7, Natick, Mass.: 1993.

Sherer, M., J. E. Maddux, B. Mercandante, S. Prentice-Dunn, B. Jacobs, and R. W. Rogers, "The Self-Efficacy Scale: Construction and Validation," *Psychological Reports*, Vol. 51, No. 2, 1982, pp. 663–671.

Shin, S. J., and J. Zhou, "When Is Educational Specialization Heterogeneity Related to Creativity in Research and Development Teams? Transformational Leadership as a Moderator," *Journal of Applied Psychology*, Vol. 92, No. 6, 2007, pp. 1709–1721.

Silvia, P. J., B. Wigert, R. Reiter-Palmon, and J. C. Kaufman, "Assessing Creativity with Self-Report Scales: A Review and Empirical Evaluation," *Psychology of Aesthetics, Creativity, and the Arts*, Vol. 6, 2012, pp. 19–34.

Smith, E. M., J. K. Ford, and S. W. J. Kozlowski, "Building Adaptive Expertise: Implications for Training Design Strategies," in M. A. Quiñones and A. Ehrenstein, eds., *Training for a Rapidly Changing Workplace*, Washington, D.C.: American Psychological Association, 1997, pp. 89–118.

Snyder, C., "The Past and Possible Futures of Hope," *Journal of Social and Clinical Psychology*, Vol. 19, No. 1, 2000, pp. 11–29.

Society for Industrial and Organizational Psychology, *Industrial and Organizational Psychology*, Vol. 3, No. 2, June 2010.

Solinger, O. N., W. van Olffen, and R. A. Roe, "Beyond the Three-Component Model of Organizational Commitment," *Journal of Applied Psychology*, Vol. 93, 2008, pp. 70–83.

Sonenshein, S., "The Role of Construction, Intuition, and Justification in Responding to Ethical Issues at Work: The Sensemaking-Intuition Model," *Academy of Management Review*, Vol. 32, No. 4, 2007, pp. 1022–1040.

Sosik, J. J., J. Juzbasich, and J. U. Chun, "Effects of Moral Reasoning and Management Level on Ratings of Charismatic Leadership, In-Role and Extra-Role Performance of Managers: A Multi-Source Examination," *The Leadership Quarterly*, Vol. 22, No. 2, 2011, pp. 434–450.

Spearman, C., "General Intelligence, Objectively Determined and Measured," *American Journal of Psychology*, Vol. 15, 1904, pp. 201–293.

Spector, P. E., and H. M. Johnson, "Improving the Definition, Measurement, and Application of Emotional Intelligence," in K. R. Murphy, ed., *A Critique of Emotional Intelligence: What Are the Problems and How Can They Be Fixed?* Mahwah, N.J.: Erlbaum, 2006, pp. 325–344.

Sprenger, A. M., S. M. Atkins, D. J. Bolger, J. I. Harbison, J. M. Novick, M. F. Bunting, and M. R. Dougherty, "Training Working Memory: Limits of Transfer," *Intelligence*, Vol. 41, 2013, pp. 638–663.

Srivastava, S., O. P. John, S. D. Gosling, and J. Potter, "Development of Personality in Early and Middle Adulthood: Set like Plaster or Persistent Change?," *Journal of Personality and Social Psychology*, Vol. 84, No. 5, 2003, pp. 1041–1053.

Stanovich, K. E., and P. J. Stanovich, "A Framework for Critical Thinking, Rational Thinking, and Intelligence," *Innovations in Educational Psychology: Perspectives on Learning, Teaching and Human Development*, 2010, pp. 195–237.

Stanovich, K. E., and R. F. West, "Individual Differences in Rational Thought," *Journal of Experimental Psychology*, Vol. 127, No. 2, 1998, pp. 161–188.

Stark, S., O. S. Chernyshenko, F. Drasgow, C. D. Nye, L. A. White, T. Heffner, and W. L. Farmer, "From ABLE to TAPAS: A New Generation of Personality Tests to Support Military Selection and Classification Decisions," *Military Psychology*, Vol. 26, No. 3, 2014, pp. 153–164.

Sternberg, D. A., K. Ballard, J. L. Hardy, B. Katz, P. M. Doraiswamy, and M. Scanlon, "The Largest Human Cognitive Performance Dataset Reveals Insights into the Effects of Lifestyle Factors and Aging," *Frontiers in Human Neuroscience*, Vol. 7, 2013, pp. 1–10.

Sternberg, R. J., *Beyond IQ: A Triarchic Theory of Human Intelligence*. New York: Cambridge University Press, 1985.

———, "Intelligence as Developing Expertise," *Contemporary Educational Psychology*, Vol. 24, No. 4, 1999, pp. 359–375.

———, "Increasing Fluid Intelligence Is Possible after All," *Proceedings of the National Academy of Sciences of the United States of America*, Vol. 105, No. 19, May 13, 2008, pp. 6791–6792.

Sternberg, R. J., and P. A. Frensch, "On Being an Expert: A Cost-Benefit Analysis," in R. R. Hoffman, ed., *The Psychology of Expertise*, New York: Springer New York, 1992, pp. 191–203.

Sternberg, R. J., and R. K. Wagner, "The g-Ocentric View of Intelligence and Job Performance Is Wrong," *Current Directions in Psychological Science*, Vol. 2, No. 1, 1993, pp. 1–4.

Stogdill, R. M., "Leadership, Membership and Organization," *Psychological Bulletin*, Vol. 47, No. 1, 1950, pp. 1–14.

Strater, L. D., D. Jones, and M. R. Endsley, *Analysis of Infantry Situation Awareness Training Requirements*, U.S. Army Research Institute for the Behavioral and Social Sciences, Arlington, Va.: Technical Report 1123, 2001.

Straus, S. G., M. G. Shanley, C. S. Sims, B. W. Hallmark, A. R. Saavedra, S. Trent, and S. Duggan, *Innovative Leader Development: Evaluation of the U.S. Army Asymmetric Warfare Adaptive Leader Program*, Santa Monica, Calif.: RAND Corporation, RR-504-A, 2014. As of January 3, 2018: https://www.rand.org/pubs/research_reports/RR504.html

Sturman, M. C., "Searching for the Inverted U-Shaped Relationship Between Time and Performance: Meta-Analyses of the Experience/Performance, Tenure/Performance, and Age/Performance Relationships," *Journal of Management*, Vol. 29, No. 5, 2003, pp. 609–640.

Tenbrunsel, A. E., and K. Smith-Crowe, "13 Ethical Decision Making: Where We've Been and Where We're Going," *The Academy of Management Annals*, Vol. 2, No. 1, 2008, pp. 545–607.

Thoma, S. J., ed., *The Minnesota Approach to Moral Psychological Research* [special issue], *Journal of Moral Education*, Vol. 31, No. 3, 2002.

Thoma, S. J., D. Narvaez, J. Rest, and P. Derryberry, "The Distinctiveness of Moral Judgment," *Educational Psychology Review*, Vol. 11, 1999, pp. 361–376.

Tierney, P., and S. M. Farmer, "Creative Self-Efficacy Development and Creative Performance Over Time," *Journal of Applied Psychology*, Vol. 96, No. 2, 2011, pp. 277–293.

Toplak, M. E., and K. E. Stanovich, "The Domain Specificity and Generality of Disjunctive Reasoning: Searching for a Generalizable Critical Thinking Skill," *Journal of Educational Psychology*, Vol. 94, 2002, pp. 197–209.

Toplak, M. E., R. F. West, and K. E. Stanovich, "Rational Thinking and Cognitive Sophistication: Development, Cognitive Abilities, and Thinking Dispositions," *Developmental Psychology*, Vol. 50, No. 4, 2014, pp.1037–1048.

Tornau, K., and M. Frese, "Construct Clean-Up in Proactivity Research: A Meta-Analysis on the Nomological Net of Work-Related Proactivity Concepts and Their Incremental Validities," *Applied Psychology: An International Review*, Vol. 62, No. 1, 2013, pp. 44–96.

Tremble, Jr., T. R., T. D. Kane, and S. R. Stewart, *A Note on Organizational Leadership as Problem Solving*, Alexandria, Va.: Army Research Institute for the Behavioral and Social Sciences, Research Note 97-03, 1997.

Treviño, L. K., N. A. den Nieuwenboer, and J. J. Kish-Gephart, "(Un)ethical Behavior in Organizations," *Annual Review of Psychology*, Vol. 65, 2014, pp. 635–660.

Treviño, L. K., G. R. Weaver, and S. J. Reynolds, "Behavioral Ethics in Organizations: A Review," *Journal of Management*, Vol. 32, No. 6, 2006, pp. 951–990.

Tugade, M. M., B. L. Fredrickson, and L. F. Barrett, "Psychological Resilience and Positive Emotional Granularity: Examining the Benefits of Positive Emotions on Coping and Health," *Journal of Personality*, Vol. 72, No. 6, 2004, pp. 1161–1190.

Turner, N., J. Barling, O. Epitropaki, V. Butcher, and C. Milner, "Transformational Leadership and Moral Reasoning," *Journal of Applied Psychology*, Vol. 87, No. 2, 2002, pp. 304–311.

Tversky, A., and D. Kahneman, "Availability: A Heuristic for Judging Frequency and Probability," *Cognitive Psychology*, Vol. 5, No. 2, 1973, pp. 207–232.

———, "Judgment Under Uncertainty: Heuristics and Biases," *Science*, Vol. 185, No. 4157, 1974, pp. 1124–1131.

———, "Extension Versus Intuitive Reasoning: The Conjunction Fallacy in Probability Judgment," *Psychological Review*, Vol. 90, No. 4, 1983, pp. 293–315.

U.S. Department of the Army, *The Army Human Dimension Strategy: Building Cohesive Teams to Win in a Complex World*, Washington, D.C., 2015. As of October 24, 2015: http://health.mil/Reference-Center/Presentations/2015/05/12/The-Army-Human-Dimension-Strategy-2015

Van Dyne, L., and J. A. LePine, "Helping and Voice Extra-Role Behaviors: Evidence of Construct and Predictive Validity," *Academy of Management Journal*, Vol. 41, 1998, pp. 108–119.

Van Iddekinge, C. H., G. R. Ferris, and T. S. Heffner, "Test of a Multistage Model of Distal and Proximal Antecedents of Leader Performance," *Personnel Psychology*, Vol. 62, 2009, pp. 463–495.

Van Rooy, D. L., and C. Viswesvaran, "Emotional Intelligence: A Meta-Analytic Investigation of Predictive Validity and Nomological Net," *Journal of Vocational Behavior*, Vol. 65, 2004, pp. 71–95.

Vergun, David, "Despite Challenges, Army Won't Lower Enlistment Standards," Army News Service, October 27, 2017. As of December 26, 2017: http://tradocnews.org/tag/opat/

Vincent, A. S., B. P. Decker, and M. D. Mumford, "Divergent Thinking, Intelligence, and Expertise: A Test of Alternative Models," *Creativity Research Journal*, Vol. 14, No. 2, 2002, pp. 163–178.

Wagner, R. K., and R. J. Sternberg, "Practical Intelligence in Real-World Pursuits: The Role of Tacit Knowledge," *Journal of Personality and Social Psychology*, Vol. 49, No. 2, 1985, pp. 436–458.

Wagner, R. K., "Tacit Knowledge in Everyday Intelligent Behavior," *Journal of Personality and Social Psychology*, Vol. 52, No. 6, 1987, pp. 1236–1247.

Wallach, M. A., and N. Kogan, *Modes of Thinking in Young Children: A Study of the Creativity-Intelligence Distinction*, New York: Holt, Rinehart, and Winston, Inc., 1965.

Watson, G., and E. M. Glaser, *Watson-Glaser Critical Thinking Appraisal*, San Antonio, Tex.: PsychCorp, 1980.

Wechsler, D., D. L. Coalson, and S. E. Raiford, *WAIS-IV: Wechsler Adult Intelligence Scale: Fourth Edition—Technical and Interpretative Manual*, San Antonio, Tex.: NCS Pearson, 2008.

Weis, S., and H. M. Süβ, "Reviving the Search for Social Intelligence—A Multitrait-Multimethod Study of Its Structure and Construct Validity," *Personality & Individual Differences*, Vol. 42, No. 1, 2007, pp. 3–14.

Welsh, J. R., S. K. Kucinkas, and L. T. Curran, *Armed Services Vocational Battery (ASVAB): Integrative Review of Validity Studies*, Brooks AFB, Tex.: Manpower and Personnel Division, Air Force Human Resources Laboratory, AFHRL-TR-90-22, 1990.

West, R. F., M. E. Toplak, and K. E. Stanovich, "Heuristics and Biases as Measures of Critical Thinking: Associations with Cognitive Ability and Thinking Dispositions," *Journal of Educational Psychology*, Vol. 100, No. 4, 2008, pp. 930–941.

Wonderlic, Inc., *Wonderlic Contemporary Cognitive Ability Test (WPT-R) Administrator's Guide*, Vernon Hills, Ill., 2012.

Wong, C., and K. S. Law, "The Effects of Leader and Follower Emotional Intelligence on Performance and Attitude: An Exploratory Study," *The Leadership Quarterly*, Vol. 13, 2002, pp. 243–274.

Wright, T. A., "A Look at Two Methodological Challenges for Scholars Interested in Positive Organizational Behavior," in D. L. Nelson and C. L. Cooper, eds., *Positive Organizational Behavior*, London: Sage Publications, 2007, pp. 177–190.

Yukl, G., and R. Mahsud, "Why Flexible and Adaptive Leadership Is Essential," *Consulting Psychology Journal: Practice and Research*, Vol. 62, No. 2, 2010, pp. 81–93.

Zaccaro, S. J., *The Nature of Executive Leadership: A Conceptual and Empirical Analysis of Success*, Washington, D.C.: American Psychological Association, 2001.

———, "Trait-Based Perspectives of Leadership," *American Psychologist*, Vol. 62, No. 1, 2007.

Zaccaro, S. J., D. Banks, L. Kiechel-Koles, C. Kemp, and P. Bader, *Leader and Team Adaptation: The Influences and Development of Key Attributes and Processes*, Arlington, Va.: U.S. Army Research Institute for the Behavioral and Social Sciences, Technical Report 1256, 2009.

Zaccaro, S. J., R. J. Foti, and D. A. Kenny, "Self-Monitoring and Trait-Based Variance in Leadership: An Investigation of Leader Flexibility across Multiple Group Situations," *Journal of Applied Psychology*, Vol. 76, No. 2, 1991, pp. 308–315.

Zaccaro, S. J., J. A. Gilbert, K. K. Thor, and M. D. Mumford, "Leadership and Social Intelligence: Linking Social Perspectiveness and Behavioral Flexibility to Leader Effectiveness," *The Leadership Quarterly*, Vol. 2, 1991, pp. 317–342.

Zaccaro, S. J., C. Kemp, and P. Bader, "Leader Traits and Attributes," in J. Antonakis, A. T. Cianciolo, and R. J. Sternberg, eds., *The Nature of Leadership*, Thousand Oaks, Calif.: Sage, 2004, pp.101–124.

Zaccaro, S. J., M. D. Mumford, M. S. Connelly, M. A. Marks, and J. A. Gilbert, "Assessment of Leader Problem-Solving Capabilities," *The Leadership Quarterly*, Vol. 11, No. 1, 2000, pp. 37–64.

Zhang, X., and J. Zhou, "Empowering Leadership, Uncertainty Avoidance, Trust, and Employee Creativity: Interaction Effects and a Mediating Mechanism," *Organizational Behavior and Human Decision Processes*, Vol. 124, 2014, pp. 150–164.

Zhao, H. A. O., S. J. Wayne, B. C. Glibkowski, and J. Bravo, "The Impact of Psychological Contract Breach on Work-Related Outcomes: A Meta-Analysis," *Personnel Psychology*, Vol. 60, No. 3, 2007, pp. 647–680.